LONDON

Compact Guide: London is the ultimate quick-reference guide to this ever-changing city, written by people who live there. It tells you all you need to know about its attractions, from Big Ben to the British Museum, from Harrods to Hyde Park, from Piccadilly Circus to Portobello Road.

This is one of 133 Compact Guides, combining the interests and enthusiasms of two of the world's best-known information providers: Insight Guides, whose innovative titles have set the standard for visual travel guides since 1970, and Discovery Channel, the world's premier source of nonfiction television programming.

D1010222

APA PUBLICATIONS

Part of the Langenscheidt Publishing Group

Insight Compact Guide: London

Edited by Brian Bell
Principal photography by Glyn Genin
Additional photography by Bill Wassman, Britta Jaschinski, Natasha Babaian, Topham Picturepoint, Bridgeman Art Library, Douglas Ward, Tony Halliday, Victoria and Albert Museum, Science & Society Picture Library, Natural History Museum, Tate London, Bill Varie/Corbis, courtesy of British Museum, Gilbert Collection, London Transport Museum, Madame Tussaud's, Geffrye Museum, Historical Royal Palaces, Bank of England Museum, Sherlock Holmes Museum, White Cube2, Pollock's Toy Museum, Shakespeare's Globe, and Deidi van Schwaenen/Dennis Severs' House.
Cover picture by: A.J. Stirling/Taxi/Getty Images
Maps: Maria Randell

NO part of this book may be reproduced, stored in a retrieval system or transmitted in any form or by any means (electronic, mechanical, photocopying, recording or otherwise), without prior written permission of *Apa Publications*. Brief text quotations with use of photographs are exempted for book review purposes only.

CONTACTING THE EDITORS: As every effort is made to provide accurate information in this publication, we would appreciate it if readers would call our attention to any errors and omissions by contacting:
Apa Publications, PO Box 7910, London SE1 1WE, England.
Fax: (44 20) 7403 0290. e-mail: insight@apaguide.co.uk

Information has been obtained from sources believed to be reliable, but its accuracy and completeness, and the opinions based thereon, are not guaranteed.

© 2004 APA Publications GmbH & Co. Verlag KG Singapore Branch, Singapore.
Maps reproduced by permission of Geographers' A-Z Map Co. Ltd. Licence No. B2589
© Crown Copyright 2004. All rights reserved. Licence number 100017302

First Edition 1995. Fourth Edition 2003. Updated 2004

Printed in Singapore by Insight Print Services (Pte) Ltd

Distributed in the UK & Ireland by:
GeoCenter International Ltd
The Viables Centre, Harrow Way, Basingstoke,
Hampshire RG22 4BJ
Tel: (44 1256) 817 987, Fax: (44 1256) 817 988

Distributed in the United States by:
Langenscheidt Publishers, Inc.
46–35 54th Road, Maspeth, NY 11378
Tel: (1 718) 784 0055, Fax: (1 718) 784 0640

Worldwide distribution enquiries:
APA Publications GmbH & Co. Verlag KG (Singapore Branch)
38 Joo Koon Road, Singapore 628990
Tel: (65) 6865 1600, Fax: (65) 6861 6438

www.insightguides.com

London

Telephone numbers: *if calling from other parts of the UK, dial 020 before the 8-digit numbers shown in this book. If calling from outside the country, use the code 44 (for the UK), then 20.*

△ **Hyde Park (p46)**
London's largest public
park is also the venue for
high-profile events.

◁ **British Museum
(p60)** From mummies
to microchips, a truly
great treasurehouse.

▽ **St Paul's Cathedral
(p26)** Christopher Wren's
masterpiece, at one end
of the Millennium Bridge.

△ **The Houses of
Parliament (p19)**
A Gothic building for
some Gothic politics.

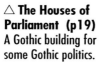

▽ **Covent Garden
(p31)** Diversions galore
where My Fair Lady used
to sell her flowers.

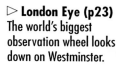

▷ **London Eye (p23)** The world's biggest observation wheel looks down on Westminster.

△ **Tower of London (p70)** The capital's top military monument for more than 900 years.

▷ **Madame Tussaud's (p58)** David Beckham scores highly in the world's most popular waxworks.

△ **National Gallery (p33)** The country's outstanding collection of Old Masters, from the early Renaissance onwards.

▷ **Tate Modern (p26)** The former power station by the Thames that generated an unprecedented interest in modern art.

Walking with History

London, it's sometimes said, is as unrepresentative of the United Kingdom as New York is of the United States. There's some truth in this. Both cities have astonishingly cosmopolitan populations, their restaurants are almost as diverse as their immigrants, they are important centres of international finance, and their range of shops and theatres is absurdly disproportionate to their size.

But London is umbilically linked to the rest of Britain in some crucial respects. Unlike New York, it is a capital city, spawning governmental institutions and corporate bureaucracies. It is also an ancient city, dating back to Roman times. Foreign forces have not occupied it since the Normans arrived in 1066 and, although it was relentlessly bombed during World War II, most of its iconic buildings survived. As a result, it exudes a palpable sense of the nation's history. You can walk in the footsteps of Shakespeare, or Dickens, or Churchill. You can journey along the Thames, as Henry VIII did. You can visit the room in the Tower of London where Sir Francis Drake lived out his last days. You can drink in the pubs where Dr Samuel Johnson drank in the 18th century.

AN UNPLANNED CITY

As visitors unwise enough to try navigating around the city by car soon discover, London is not uniform. It is patchy, unplanned, organic. This is not a city of grand vistas, but everyone finds his or her own favourite holes and corners. While it has a long and venerable past, that past is often not visible. Over the centuries the ripples of history have repeatedly destroyed parts of the city and the subsequent rebuilding has resulted in a cocktail of streets that combine many different tastes.

Queen Boudicca burnt the the city the Romans had built here in AD 61, but this was just the first of many serious setbacks. The plagues of 1665 claimed the lives of 100,000 Londoners and a year

> **A heavyweight city**
> London has always been dominant within Great Britain. In 1605, 6 percent of the country's population lived in the city. Today more than 7 million people – 12 percent of the population – reside in the metropolis. It's cosmopolitan, too: one in three of those residents is from a minority ethnic group.

Opposite: the British Museum's Great Court
Below: Tower Bridge opens to let a cruise ship pass through

Below: statue of Sir Francis Drake at Greenwich
Bottom: Winston Churchill's statue overlooking Big Ben

later the Great Fire, started in Pudding Lane, destroyed much of the city. In the bombing blitz of World War II, 29,000 Londoners were killed, and 80 percent of buildings in the City (the financial area) were damaged, a third destroyed.

In this process of change, something good has usually emerged from each disaster. So dark and narrow were the streets in the old City of London, for example, that shopkeepers had to erect mirrors outside their windows to reflect light into the shops. The heavy bombing of World War II eventually provided the opportunity for widening and lightening; slums disappeared and the level of street crime declined.

CITY OF SURPRISES

Every now and then the city becomes brazenly fashionable – the Swinging London of the 1960s, for instance, or 'the coolest place on the planet', as *Newsweek* dubbed it in the 1990s – but what attracts millions of visitors, year in and year out, is less the sparkling baubles of popular culture than the crown jewels of continuity and tradition. It's a patchy, unplanned city and you never know what you are going to find around the next corner – gothic carvings adorning a Victorian office block, a narrow alley that has defied redevelopers for seven centuries, a blue plaque on the wall of an ordinary looking house testifying that Benjamin Franklin, Florence Nightingale, Karl Marx or Jimi Hendrix once lived here.

The immensity of the place makes it hard to embrace as a whole and you don't find long-time residents proclaiming their feelings through 'I ❤ London' stickers. Many people seldom venture into the West End and identify instead with their local communities such as Notting Hill, or Hampstead, or Brixton, or Dulwich – hence the saying that London is really a collection of 'villages', once independent but long since swallowed up by the metropolis. Each of these villages has a separate 'feel', and the most interesting are covered in this book.

POPULATION AND SIZE

After decades of decline, London's population has increased since the mid-1980s to its present 7.2 million and forecasts show it surging to almost 8 million by 2016. More than one in three residents is from a minority ethnic group, and around 300 languages are spoken (from Abem, a language of the Ivory Coast, to Zulu, from South Africa). More than 250,000 refugees have come to London over the past 15 years and a higher percentage of Indian and Pakistanis now own their own homes in the capital than white people. Service industries such as catering and hospitals rely heavily on immigrant labour. Prosperity ranges from the billionaires of Belgravia to the down-and-outs sleeping rough in shop doorways.

Officially, London's area is 610 sq. miles (1,580 sq. km), but the urban sprawl around the capital makes it hard to know where to stop measuring.

CLIMATE

The climate in London is mild, with the warming effects of the city itself keeping off the worst of the cold in winter. Snow and temperatures below freezing are unusual, with January temperatures averaging 43°F/6°C. Temperatures in the summer months average 64°F/18°C, but they can soar, causing the city to become airlessly hot (air-conditioning is not universal).

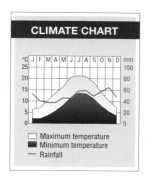

CLIMATE CHART

☐ Maximum temperature
■ Minimum temperature
– Rainfall

Below: souvenirs of London
Bottom: cruising on the river

However, temperatures can fluctuate considerably from day to day and surprise showers catch people unawares all year round. Therefore visitors should come prepared with wet-weather clothes, whatever the season. Generally speaking, short sleeves and a jacket are fine for summer, but a warm coat and woollens are needed in winter. Predicting tomorrow's weather is riskier than roulette.

GOVERNMENT

In 1986 Margaret Thatcher's Conservative government, tiring of the left-wing policies of the Greater London Council and its leader, Ken Livingstone, abolished it. This draconian action left London's government balkanised between the existing 32 local boroughs and the Corporation of London (whose Lord Mayor and councillors run the financial square mile known as the City of London). The most conspicuous victim of this lack of central planning was transport: traffic congestion slowed down bus services and the Underground's infrastructure and rolling stock continued to deteriorate because of lack of investment.

Tony Blair's Labour government, elected in 1997, decided to restore a measure of local government by creating a Greater London Authority under the direction of a mayor – a new post for London and distinct from the centuries-old post of Lord Mayor who presides over the Corpora-

Below: City Hall, near Tower Bridge
Bottom: London, as seen from the top of St Paul's Cathedral, is a relatively low-rise city

tion of London's administration. Although Blair did everything possible to stop the maverick Ken Livingstone becoming mayor, the voters decisively elected him. Four bodies eat up most of the GLA's budget: the Metropolitan Police Authority, the London Fire and Emergency Planning Authority, the London Development Agency and Transport for London.

Local services such as refuse disposal, housing grants and parking control are still run by the 32 boroughs: Barking, Barnet, Bexley, Brent, Bromley, Camden, Croydon, Ealing, Enfield, Greenwich, Hackney, Hammersmith and Fulham, Haringey, Harrow, Havering, Hillingdon, Hounslow, Islington, Kensington and Chelsea, Kingston-upon-Thames, Lambeth, Lewisham, Merton, Newham, Redbridge, Richmond-upon-Thames, Southwark, Sutton, Tower Hamlets, Waltham Forest, Wandsworth, and Westminster.

THE POLICE

The Metropolitan Police Force was founded in 1829 by prime minister Sir Robert Peel, hence the nicknames 'bobbies' and 'peelers'. It employs 25,500 officers and 10,800 civilian staff, but the high cost of living in London makes recruiting a problem. A separate force of City of London Police covers the financial district, and the British Transport Police concentrate on buses, trains and the Underground.

TRANSPORT

Although an efficient Underground (the 'Tube') is the best antidote to the capital's traffic congestion, there is no consensus on how to run it. The mayor, Ken Livingstone, appointed as traffic commissioner Bob Kiley, who was credited with transforming New York's subway, and together they advocated regenerating the crumbling Tube network by issuing bonds. But the Blair government insisted that the Tube should be rebuilt using a mixture of public and private investment, and this stalemate halted progress. Livingstone concentrated on providing more buses and bus lanes, and in 2003 imposed a £5 'congestion

Quotable London

James Boswell, quoting Dr Samuel Johnson in 1777: 'Why, Sir, you find no man, at all intellectual, who is willing to leave London. No, Sir, when a man is tired of London, he is tired of life; for there is in London all that life can afford.'

Hell is a city much like London
A populous and smoky city.
— Percy Bysshe Shelley, 1819

London is a roost for every bird.
— Benjamin Disraeli, 1870

One of the charms of London is that there are no Londoners.
— H.V. Morton, 1929

When it's three o'clock in New York, it's still 1938 in London.
— Bette Midler, 1978

The classic Routemaster bus

Telephone boxes

When British Telecom was privatised, the newly profit-conscious managers began to replace the old small-paned red telephone boxes with modern, low-maintenance kiosks. Traditionalists – and tourism officials – erupted and the red icons were reinstated. Fewer are needed now, thanks to the growth of mobile phones, but they still provide a handy (if illegal) place to display cards advertising the varied services of call-girls.

Below: taxi outside Harrods
Bottom: old-style phone boxes

charge' on anyone driving into central London during working hours.

THE LONDON TAXI

About 20,000 drivers work in London, half of them as owner-drivers. The others either hire vehicles from the big fleets or work night shifts in someone else's cab. In all, there are more than 15,000 vehicles. The classic cab, the FX4, was launched in 1959 and some models are still going strong. The newer Metrocab is more spacious.

Would-be drivers must register with the Public Carriage Office and then spend up to four years learning London in minute detail (called 'doing the Knowledge'). They achieve this by travelling the streets of the metropolis on a moped, whatever the weather, working out a multitude of routes from a clipboard mounted on the handlebars. Even though the allegedly garrulous cabbies may not always know what they're talking about, they do know where they're going.

THE COCKNEY

The original definition of a cockney – someone born within the sound of Bow bells, the clarion of St Mary-le-Bow in Cheapside in the City – would today exclude most Londoners. The resident population of the City (London's financial area) is tiny, and the sound does not penetrate far. Also, cockneys no longer need to be white and Anglo-Saxon; there are Italian, West Indian, Jewish and Pakistani cockneys. So what then makes a cockney? Certain traditions, being a member of an identifiable urban group, a distinctive language – and a quick sense of humour.

Cockney is a London accent, widely broadcast by 'Enry 'Iggins in the musical *My Fair Lady*. It has no use of the aspirant 'h', the 't' in the middle of words such as 'butter', or the final 'g' in words ending 'ing'. Cockneys traditionally speak in a rhyming slang which supposedly originated among barrow boys who didn't want their customers to understand what they said to each other. A 'whistle' is a suit, short for whistle and flute, and 'trouble and strife' means wife.

THE ROYALS

Pageantry such as the Changing of the Guard is concentrated at Buckingham Palace, even though the Queen spends part of the year at her other residences, such as Windsor Castle, Sandringham in Norfolk, or Balmoral in Scotland. Other royals live elsewhere in London – at Kensington Palace, for example, and St James's Palace.

Below: the Albert Memorial in Kensington Gardens
Bottom: the Guards step out

Amost every day of the year, a member of the Royal Family appears in public somewhere in London, pursued by battalions of royalty watchers, professional and amateur. As patrons of many societies, the members of the family are in demand to open buildings, give prizes and visit hospitals. The Court Circular, published daily in major national newspapers, details their engagements.

On the second Saturday in June, when the Queen's birthday is officially celebrated, she travels by carriage to Horse Guards Parade for the ceremony of Trooping the Colour. In November, she is transported by state coach to Westminster for the State Opening of Parliament, escorted along the Mall by the Household Cavalry and greeted by a fanfare of trumpets. This is the only time she wears the monarch's traditional robes and crown. Also in November, she attends the Service of Remembrance at the Cenotaph in Whitehall. In July a member of the family takes the salute at the Royal Tournament, a military show at Earl's Court.

HISTORICAL HIGHLIGHTS

AD43 Londinium is settled during the second Roman invasion; a bridge is built over the Thames.

61 Boudicca, Queen of the Iceni tribe in East Anglia, sacks the city before being defeated and killed.

c.200 Three-mile (5-km) city wall built, encompassing a fort, forum, amphitheatre and temple.

410 Troops withdrawn to defend Rome.

604 St Paul's Cathedral is founded by King Ethelbert.

c750 Monastery of St Peter is founded on Thorney Island, and later becomes Westminster Abbey.

8th century Shipping and manufacturing flourish on the Thames riverbank.

884 London becomes the country's capital under Alfred the Great.

1042 Edward the Confessor moves his court from the city to Westminster and rebuilds the Abbey.

1066 William I, Duke of Normandy and descendant of the Vikings who settled in northern France, conquers Britain and is crowned king. The Normans introduce French and the feudal system.

1078 The Tower of London's White Tower is built to intimidate enemies.

1176 London Bridge is built of stone.

1191 The City elects its first mayor.

1220 St Paul's Cathedral is rebuilt.

1444 The Guildhall is rebuilt.

1514 Hampton Court Palace is begun.

1532 Henry VIII builds the Palace of Whitehall, the largest royal edifice in Europe. It catches fire in 1698.

1534 Henry VIII declares himself head of the Church of England and dissolves the monasteries.

1536 St James's Palace is built.

1550 Somerset House is built.

1588 William Shakespeare (1568–1616) begins his dramatic career in London.

1605 Guy Fawkes tries to blow up Parliament; he is caught and executed.

1620 Pilgrim Fathers sail to America.

1642–49 Civil war between the Cavalier Royalists and the republican Roundheads. Royalists are defeated. Charles I is executed.

1660 Monarchy restored under Charles II.

1660–69 Samuel Pepys (1633–1703) writes his diary chronicling contemporary events.

1664–66 The Great Plague kills one-fifth of the 500,000 population.

1666 The Great Fire destroys 80 percent of London's mostly wooden buildings.

1675 Sir Christopher Wren (1632–1723) starts work on St Paul's Cathedral.

1694 The Bank of England is established.

1699 St James's Palace is used as a royal court, and continues to be so for the next 138 years.

1724 St Martin-in-the-Fields is built.

1732 George II makes 10 Downing Street available to Sir Robert Walpole, Britain's first Prime Minister; it is established as the home of future premiers.

1744 Sotheby's auction house founded.

1764 The Literary Club is founded by Dr Samuel Johnson, the compiler of the first English dictionary.

1783 Last public execution at Tyburn.

1811–20 The Prince Regent, later to become George IV, gives his name to the Regency style.

1820 Regent's Canal is completed.

1824 The National Gallery is established.

1829 A prototype police force ('peelers') is established by Robert Peel.

1834 The Houses of Parliament are built after the Old Palace of Westminster is destroyed by fire.

1840s Trafalgar Square is laid out on the site of royal stables to commemorate Admiral Lord Nelson's victory.

1851 Great Exhibition held in Hyde Park.

1859 A 13-ton bell, Big Ben, is hung in the Houses of Parliament's Clock Tower.

1863 The first section of the Underground railway is built between Paddington and Farringdon Street.

1888 A serial murderer known as Jack the Ripper strikes in Whitechapel.

1890 The first electric railway to be built in deep-level tunnels begins operating between the City and Stockwell.

1894 Tower Bridge is built.

1903 Westminster Cathedral is built.

1909 The Victoria and Albert Museum opens in South Kensington.

1914 World War I begins. First air raids.

1922 British Broadcasting Company transmits its first radio programmes.

1939–45 World War II. Children are evacuated, London is heavily bombed. 29,000 civilians are killed and 1.75 million London homes destroyed.

1951 Festival of Britain includes the building of new concert halls on the South Bank near Waterloo.

1956 Passing of the Clean Air Act brings an end to the asphyxiating smogs.

1976 National Theatre building opened.

1982 Thames Barrier is completed.

1986 The Greater London Council, the ruling city authority, is abolished.

1991 Canary Wharf tower is completed.

1996 Shakespeare's Globe, a replica of the original theatre burnt down in 1599, opens on Bankside.

2000 Millennium Dome opens at Greenwich and the London Eye at County Hall.

2001 Greater London Authority is set up under new mayor Ken Livingstone.

2002 Millennium Bridge reopens after its notorious 'wobble' is cured.

2003 A 'congestion charge' of £5 a day is imposed on cars entering central London during weekday working hours.

Map below

1: Westminster Abbey to St Paul's Cathedral

Westminster Abbey – Parliament – South Bank – Tate Modern – St Paul's Cathedral

Preceding pages: the Thames as seen from the London Eye

This route, 2½ miles (4km) long, is a general introduction to London. It combines ancient and modern, sacred and secular, and twice crosses the Thames, the river around which the city grew.

> **St Margaret's Church**
> This church (which, unlike the abbey, has free admission) faces the Houses of Parliament. Rebuilt in 1486–1523, it contains stained-glass tributes to Henry VIII, printer William Caxton (buried here in 1491), explorer Sir Walter Raleigh and writer John Milton (1608–74).

WESTMINSTER ABBEY

The route begins at ★★★**Westminster Abbey ❶**, Britain's most historic religious building. It is also a fine piece of Gothic architecture, which is probably more striking for the intricate detail on the inside than from its relatively plain outward aspects. Much of the

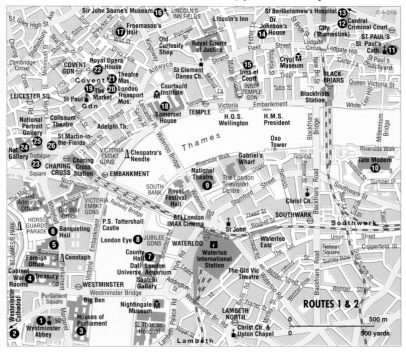

ROUTES 1 & 2

500 m

500 yards

present abbey, the third on the site, was built in the 13th century in early English Gothic-style by Henry III. During the 16th century, Henry VII added on the remarkable chapel at the eastern end of the sanctuary in the late Gothic Perpendicular style. During the 18th century, Nicholas Hawksmoor designed the distinctive towers at the main west entrance.

Until the 16th century the abbey was an important monastery. Henry VIII dissolved the monasteries in 1534 when he quarrelled with the Pope, who refused to allow him to divorce, but Westminster Abbey continued to be used as the royal church for coronations and burials. All but two of the reigning monarchs from William the Conqueror in 1066 were crowned here, and the Abbey houses the English Coronation Chair, built in 1300 for Edward I.

So many eminent figures have been honoured in this national shrine that extensive areas of the interior have the cluttered and confused appearance of an overcrowded sculpture museum. The Tomb of the Unknown Warrior houses the body of a soldier brought back from France after World War I as an anonymous representative of the countless dead.

Poets' Corner lies beyond the nave in the south transept. Geoffrey Chaucer was the first poet to be buried here, in 1400. Other literary figures here include Alfred Lord Tennyson; the poet and dramatist Ben Jonson, who is buried standing upright; William Shakespeare, John Milton, John Keats and Oscar Wilde. Behind the sanctuary are magnificent and ornate royal chapels and tombs.

The Abbey should not be confused with ★**Westminster Cathedral ❷**, which lies at the other end of Victoria Street. This sumptuous Italian-Byzantine building is the most important Roman Catholic church in London. There are good views from a gallery atop its 330-ft (100-metre) striped tower.

HOUSES OF PARLIAMENT

Facing the Abbey, the clock tower of the ★★**Houses of Parliament ❸** has become a symbol of the city. Its elaborately fretted stone sides rise nearly 330 ft (100 metres) to a richly gilded spire above the clock and a 13-ton hour bell supposedly nicknamed **Big**

Star attractions
● **Westminster Abbey**
● **Houses of Parliament**

Below: Westminster Abbey
Bottom: Westminster Cathedral

Map on page 18

Big Ben
The first great bell to adorn the rebuilt Palace of Westminster's clock tower was made in the north of England and brought to London by sea in 1856. But a heavy clapper cracked the 16-ton bell, dubbed Big Ben. Its metal was broken up and used to recast a lighter bell in a foundry in Whitechapel, east London. The 2½-ton cast-iron hands were then found to be too heavy to move, and hollow minute hands were designed.

Ben after a plump government official called Sir Benjamin Hall who was commissioner of works when the bell was installed.

The oldest part of Parliament is Westminster Hall, begun in 1078. The thick buttressed walls are spanned with a magnificent hammer-beamed oak roof. Among those condemned to death here were King Charles I, accused of treason against Parliament; and the 17th-century revolutionary Guy Fawkes, who tried to blow up the buildings.

In 1835 a fire achieved what Guy Fawkes had failed to do and most of the ancient rambling Palace of Westminster was destroyed. Westminster Hall and a small crypt chapel survived. The present Houses of Parliament were created in an exuberant Gothic style by Sir Charles Barry and Augustus Pugin. The immense Victoria Tower marks the southern end of the building, and the grand entrance to the House of Lords. A Union Flag (the national flag, colloquially called the Union Jack) flies from the tower when parliament is in session. Night sittings are indicated by a light shining over the clock tower.

The building covers 8 acres (3.2 hectares); there are 11 open courtyards and more than 1,100 rooms. Apart from the ceremonial state rooms and the two main debating chambers, the House of Lords and the House of Commons, there are libraries, dining rooms, tea rooms and offices. Many of the walls are covered with heroic Victorian paintings and the

Big Ben is the name of the main bell, not the clock tower

woodwork is carved in an intricate Gothic fashion. Anyone can watch debates from the visitors' gallery, providing they start queueing early enough.

Star attraction
● **Cabinet War Rooms**

CABINET WAR ROOMS

Across Parliament Square, at the end of Clive Steps which lead off King Charles Street, the fascinating ★★**Cabinet War Rooms** ❹ (open daily 9.30am–5pm; entrance fee) sheltered the government during World War II and include the combined office-bedroom used by Sir Winston Churchill. Many of the 21 rooms were simply abandoned in 1945 and were left untouched until the museum opened in 1984; many that were cleared out have been meticulously restored to their wartime condition, 'down to the last paper clip', using old photographs for reference, and more are being opened. A handheld audio guide provides a commentary in eight languages.

Below: statue of Clive of India at the top of Clive Steps
Bottom: Winston Churchill at the Cabinet War Rooms

The Cabinet Room is set up as it would have been for a meeting in 1940, with the red box used to carry State papers sitting in front of Churchill's distinctive chair at the top table. The Map Room and the rooms that served as round-the-clock typing pools illustrate forcefully the gulf between communications in the 1940s and today's VDU-filled world. A converted broom cupboard housed a pioneering 'hot line' to the White House, enabling Churchill to have confidential talks with President Franklin D. Roosevelt. Displays include a selection of weapons owned by Churchill and selections of his letters and telegrams.

DOWNING STREET

If you return to the end of King Charles Street, the **Cenotaph**, the national war memorial designed by Sir Edward Lutyens, is to your left and, beyond it, to the left off Whitehall, is ★**Downing Street** ❺, where the Prime Minister lives at Number 10. Security precautions prevent you entering the street, but you can gaze through gates.

Further along Whitehall, the ★**Banqueting Hall** ❻ (Mon–Sat 10am–5pm, fee), built by Inigo

Map on page 18

Seeds of history
For 800 years the London residence of the once powerful Archbishops of Canterbury has sat across the Thames within sight of Parliament. The medieval **Lambeth Palace** is not open to the public, but a former church in its shadow by Lambeth Bridge is a **Museum of Garden History** (Sun–Fri 10.30am–5pm, closed mid-Dec to Feb). The adjacent churchyard contains the grave of Captain William Bligh of the *Bounty*.

Jones in 1622, is still used for receptions. The Great Hall's splendid painted ceiling is the only complete project by Peter Paul Rubens still *in situ*.

If you wish to visit ★★**Tate Britain**, the country's main collection of British art *(see page 99)*, proceed westwards along the Thames for about 15 minutes, past Lambeth Bridge.

COUNTY HALL'S ATTRACTIONS

Head back to Big Ben and cross Westminster Bridge (built 1854–62), passing the imposing statue of Queen Boudicca in her chariot; she was the warrior who tried to drive the Romans from Britain in the 1st century AD. At the southern end, the imposing building in Edwardian Renaissance style is **County Hall ❼**. Completed in 1922, it was the headquarters of the London County Council and its successor, the Greater London Council, until the left-leaning GLC was abolished by Margaret Thatcher's government in 1986. Japan's Shirayama Shokusan Corporation, which bought the majestic building for £60 million, divided it between an upmarket hotel (Marriott), a utilitarian hotel (Travel Inn), an aquarium, an art gallery, a games arcade and a branch of McDonald's.

The central attraction is the ★★**London Aquarium** (daily 10am–6pm, fee). A gently descending route, ideal for wheelchairs and pushchairs,

County Hall, with pods of the London Eye in the foreground

winds through seven different aquatic environments on three levels, beginning with freshwater stream, voyaging through the world's great oceans and ending with coral reefs, rainforest and mangrove swamps. Thousands of specimens representing 350 species of fish inhabit over 440,000 gallons (2 million litres) of mains-fed but specially treated water. Atmospheric sounds, smells and lighting are effectively deployed. It is worth catching the shark and rainforest talks (tel: 7967 8029 for schedule) and feed times (shark feeding Tues, Thurs, Sat 2.30pm; piranha feeding, in Tropical Freshwater, Mon, Wed, Fri and Sun 1pm), when divers dish out mackerel and squid.

Beside the aquarium, **Namco Station** is an interactive neon-lit entertainment centre with ear-bashing music and the latest Playstation and video games. There are also bumper cars, a bowling alley, fantastic simulators, and fruit machines.

The **Dalí Universe** (daily 10am–5.30pm; fee) has more than 500 of Salvador Dalí's surreal works on show. They're not his best creations but will be of interest to Dalí enthusiasts.

THE LONDON EYE

Towering incongruously over County Hall is the **★★London Eye ❽**, the world's largest observation wheel, built to mark the millennium. The statistics alone impress. At 450 ft (135 metres), it is the fourth highest structure in London. The hub and spindle weigh 330 tonnes – heavier than 40 double-decker buses. The 32 fully enclosed capsules, each holding 25 people, take 30 minutes to make a full rotation – a speed slow enough to allow passengers to step in and out of the capsules while the wheel keeps moving. On a clear day, you can see for 25 miles (40 km).

Visitors can be left with an impression of an incoherent, surprisingly low-rise urban sprawl with quite a lot of green space. Certainly it's clear that the city is resolutely unplanned.

To avoid queues at peak periods, you can make an automated telephone booking on 0870 5000 600 (but check the weather forecast first).

Star attractions
● **Tate Britain**
● **London Aquarium**
● **London Eye**

Below: the London Aquarium
Bottom: the London Eye

Map on page 18

Giant screen

At Waterloo Bridge, which soars over the riverside walkway between the Hayward Gallery and the National Theatre, you can cut up to the London IMAX Cinema, part of the British Film Institute. This 482-seater cinema rests on 60 giant springs designed to eradicate vibration from tube trains running just 15 ft (4.5 metres) beneath it. Large-format film – 10 times the size of standard 35mm stock – is projected onto a screen 66 ft high by 85 ft wide (20 by 26 metres). The 11,600-watt digital surround-sound system, using 44 speakers, is ideal for experiencing the sensation of a space shuttle blasting off from Cape Canaveral.

The London IMAX cinema

THE SOUTH BANK CENTRE

Along the river, to the east of Jubilee Gardens, is Europe's biggest arts complex. The first building, the ★**Royal Festival Hall** (RFH), is the oldest and largest of the three concert halls on the South Bank. Built on the site of the Lion Brewery, destroyed by bombing during World War II, it was opened in 1951 as part of the Festival of Britain, a celebration designed to improve the country's morale after five years of post-war austerity. In 1967 the 2,900-seat RFH gained two smaller neighbours, the **Queen Elizabeth Hall** and the **Purcell Room**. The QEH seats 917 people and is designed for chamber concerts, music theatre and opera. The 372-seater Purcell Room is intended for solo recitals and chamber music.

The halls' cafés and bars, and book and record shops are open throughout the day. The foyer of the RFH is also used as an exhibition space for sculpture, photography and painting, and free lunchtime concerts.

Tucked away in the South Bank Centre's brutalist concrete jungle between the Royal Festival Hall and the National Theatre is the **Hayward Gallery** *(see page 98)*.

Nestling almost invisibly beneath the southern end of Waterloo Bridge is the **National Film Theatre**, Britain's leading arthouse cinema. With three auditoria, the NFT holds more than 2,400

screenings and events each year, from lovingly restored silent movies (to a live piano accompaniment) to pioneering world cinema productions, to the latest Hollywood blockbuster.

Star attraction
● **National Theatre**

THE NATIONAL THEATRE

The next riverside edifice in the South Bank's relentless concrete jungle is the ★★**National Theatre** ❾ (box office: 7452 3000). It has no seasons as such; old and new plays are presented in repertoire all year. The turn-around is fast – up to nine productions in any two weeks – and the venue draws big-name actors and directors. The complex houses three theatres under one roof.

Below: secondhand bookstalls by the river at the South Bank
Bottom: the Oxo Tower

The **Olivier**, which seats up to 1,200 people, is the biggest. The design of the fan-shaped auditorium is based on the Greek amphitheatre at Epidaurus and the stage has a revolving drum with elevators that can bring scenery and props smoothly on and off the stage during performances. The **Lyttelton** is a more conventional two-tier proscenium theatre, with room for about 900 people. The smallest and most intimate of the trio is the **Cottesloe**, a rectangular room with a floor space surrounded by galleries on three sides, where both seating and stage can be rearranged to suit the play, often an experimental production.

Immediately to the east is an IBM office building and, beyond it, an 18-storey tower housing **London Weekend Television**. Then, by the river, is **Gabriel's Wharf**, a small group of single-storey buildings backed by a striking set of *trompe l'œil* paintings; speciality shops, studios and restaurants are set around an open space dotted with seating and wood carvings.

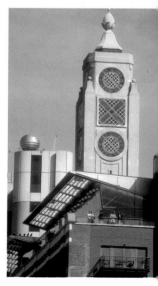

One of the South Bank's best-known landmarks is the Art Deco **Oxo Tower**. When the original owners were forbidden to advertise their leading product, the Oxo stock cube, in neon lettering, the architect devised 'an elemental geometric form' using three letters: O, X, and O as 10-ft (3-metre) high windows looking out north, south, east and west. The tower has a public viewing gallery and an upscale restaurant.

Map on page 18

The Millennium Bridge
Said to resemble a 'blade of light' when floodlit, this innovative suspension bridge – its cables are strung horizontally rather than vertically – opened in 2000. But the crowds who initially surged across it caused the bridge to sway unpredictably and it had to be closed for nearly two embarrassing years of engineering adjustments. Pedestrians can now walk without a wobble between Tate Modern and St Paul's in just seven minutes, and the views up and down river are captivating.

BANKSIDE

The riverside walkway runs under **Blackfriars Bridge**. (You can ascend to street level for a drink at London's most spectacular Arts & Crafts pub, the Black Friar.) Continuing eastward brings you to the unobtrusive **Bankside Gallery** *(see page 97)* and the very obtrusive ★★★**Tate Modern** ❿ (Sun–Thur 10am–6pm, Fri–Sat 10am–10pm; free), whose soaring chimney is a reminder that the building, incorporating more than 4 million bricks, was a power station between 1953 and 1981. The Tate spent £134 million converting it to house Britain's principal modern art collection, keeping its earlier collections across the river in Tate Britain. In its first year, from May 2000, Tate Modern attracted a remarkable 5.2 million visitors. The massive Turbine Hall is used to display large-scale installations and the exhibition rooms are spread across three levels accessible by escalator, staircase and lifts *(see page 100)*.

Further along the riverside walkway is Shakespeare's Globe *(see page 76)*, but our route takes us from Tate Modern across the Millennium Bridge *(see panel)* to St Paul's Cathedral.

ST PAUL'S CATHEDRAL

The Millennium Bridge leads to Tate Modern art gallery

★★★**St Paul's** ⓫ (Mon–Sat 8.30am–4pm; fee), the first purpose-built Protestant cathedral, is Sir

Christopher Wren's greatest work. A tablet above Wren's plain marble tomb reads: *Lector, si monumentum requiris, circumspice* (Reader, if you wish to see his memorial, look around you.)

Historians believe that the first church on the St Paul's site was built in the 7th century, although it really came into its own as Old St Paul's only in the 14th century, and by the 16th century it was the tallest cathedral in England. Much of the building was destroyed in the Great Fire of 1666. Construction on the new St Paul's Cathedral began in 1675, when Wren was 43.

The architect was an old man of 78 when his son Christopher finally laid the highest stone of the lantern on the central cupola in 1710. In total, the cathedral cost £747,954 to build, and most of the money was raised through taxing coal arriving in the port of London. The building is massive and the Portland stone dome alone – exceeded in size only by St Peter's in Rome – weighs more than 50,000 tons. Generations of schoolchildren have giggled secret messages in St Paul's Whispering Gallery, more than 100 ft (30 metres) of perfect acoustics. You have to climb 260 steps to reach it, however, and a further 270 to enjoy the tremendous view from the highest of the dome's three galleries.

Although Westminster Abbey hosts more national occasions, St Paul's still has its moments. Churchill lay in state here in 1965, and Prince Charles married Diana Spencer here in 1981.

In the Cathedral's Crypt, the largest vault of its kind in Europe, is a treasury containing gold and silver ceremonial vessels, a burial chamber and a chapel dedicated to members of the Order of the British Empire (OBE), who may be married or have members of their families baptised here. The highlights of this cavernous undercroft include the tombs of the Duke of Wellington (whose casket was so huge that it had to be lowered into its resting place via a hole in the Cathedral floor) and of Admiral Lord Nelson, who was foresighted enough to take a coffin with him to the Battle of Trafalgar. Exhibits trace the history of previous churches on the site.

Star attractions
● **Tate Modern**
● **St Paul's Cathedral**

Below: St Paul's Cathedral
Bottom: inside St Paul's

Map on page 18

Below: the statue of Justice (1907) stands atop the Central Criminal Court
Bottom: Dr Samuel Johnson as portrayed in a window of his former home off Fleet Street

2: St Paul's to Trafalgar Square

Old Bailey – Fleet Street – Royal Courts of Justice – Covent Garden – Trafalgar Square

As you walk down Ludgate Hill from St Paul's Cathedral, **Old Bailey** is on your right. The street name is also popularly used to refer to its chief building, the **Central Criminal Court** ⓬, whose domed is topped with the golden figure of Justice, a sword in her right hand and, in her left, scales to weigh the evidence. Many great murder trials have been staged here, and you can still watch dramas from the visitors' gallery (Mon–Fri 10.15am and 1.45pm, closed Aug).

To the north, in West Smithfield, is **St Bartholomew's Hospital** ⓭, London's oldest. A small museum traces its history back to the 12th century. **Smithfield meat market**, which dates to the 17th century, is active between 4am and 9am.

Cut down Farringdon Road to Ludgate Circus and up Fleet Street *(see panel)*. On the left, **St Bride's Church**, designed by Sir Christopher Wren, has a crypt containing interesting Roman artefacts found on this ancient site. The street's literary associations can be found in ★**Dr Johnson's House** ⓮ (Mon–Sat 11am–5.30pm; fee), at 17 Gough Square, where the great lexicographer lived from 1748 to 1759. Close by, in Wine Office Court, **Ye Old Cheshire Cheese** evokes the pubs of Samuel Johnson's day. On the first floor of 17 Fleet Street, **Prince Henry's Room** (Mon–Sat 11am–2pm, free) has an elaborate 17th-century plasterwork ceiling and fine wood panelling and contains artefacts and paintings relating to the diarist Samuel Pepys (1633–1703).

ROYAL COURTS OF JUSTICE

Between Fleet Street and the river are the **Inns of Court** ⓯, home to London's top lawyers. As Fleet Street becomes Strand, the neo-Gothic confection of towers and spires on the right is one of their principal stages, the Royal Courts of Justice, the venue for libels, divorces and civil cases. Visitors can sit in the public galleries of the 58 courts when trials are in session.

Two churches sit on traffic islands in Strand: the baroque **St Mary le Strand**, built in 1714, and **St Clement Danes**, begun by Wren in 1769.

RICH COLLECTIONS

Turn up the crescent of Aldwych and into Kingsway, and turn right into **Lincoln's Inn Fields**, an oasis of greenery created for the recreation of the legal students from Lincoln's Inn. Here, at number 13, is one of London's most remarkable attractions. ★★**Sir John Soane's Museum** ⑯ (Tues–Sat 10am–5pm; free) is a British Museum in miniature, an eclectic and eccentric collection assembled in his home by Soane (1753–1837), a master architect. His house and collection, including an Egyptian sarcophagus and both *The Rake's Progress* and *An Election Entertainment*, two of William Hogarth's series of caricatures, remain much as they were during his lifetime.

Return to Kingsway and cross it into Great Queen Street, where **Freemason's Hall** ⑰ (tel: 7395 9258, free) is worth seeing for its spectacular Art-Deco internal decoration. There are displays of Masonic regalia and memorabilia, but not many veils are lifted on this secretive fraternal society.

Star attraction
● **Sir John Soane's Museum**

Yesterday's news
For centuries, Fleet Street was the dynamic centre of national newspaper production. In the 1980s new technology allowed owners to build remote printing plants and move journalists to cheaper offices. No major newspaper remains on Fleet Street. Two sister papers, *The Guardian* and *The Observer*, whose offices are in nearby Farringdon Road, run a museum, **The Newsroom**, housing their archives, providing an exhibition space and allowing school groups to lay out their own front page. Details at guardian.co.uk/newsroom

William Hogarth's 'An Election Entertainment', on show at Sir John Soane's Museum

Map on page 18

Cleopatra's Needle
This 186-ton granite obelisk, 60 ft high (18 metres), was erected in 1878 on Victoria Embankment, to the west of Waterloo Bridge. Dating from before 1475BC, it was gifted to Britain by Egypt's Turkish viceroy and was towed here by sea.

Below: a Swiss snuffbox (circa 1812) in the Gilbert Collection
Bottom: Somerset House in summer

A left turn into Drury Lane takes you past the **Theatre Royal** (1663). Nell Gwynne, Charles II's mistress, trod the boards here, and today the venue is mostly used for blockbuster musicals.

On Aldwych, turn right and, at the end of the crescent you will be facing Waterloo Bridge. A short distance to its left is the main entrance to ★**Somerset House** ⑱, a magnificent 18th-century neoclassical mansion used until recent times as headquarters of the Inland Revenue. Today it is home to the Gilbert Collection and the Hermitage Exhibition (10am–6pm; fee), and its fine courtyard, once a car park, is turned into a public skating rink for several weeks in winter.

The **Gilbert Collection** consists of silver, gold and micro-mosaics (intricate pictures made from coloured stone or glass), donated to Britain in 1996 by a real-estate millionaire, Sir Arthur Gilbert. Highlights include gem-encrusted boxes that belonged to Frederick the Great.

The **Hermitage Exhibition** consists of five grand rooms hosting temporary exhibitions from the monumental St Petersburg museum; telephone 7845 4600 for details of current exhibitions.

COVENT GARDEN

Continue west along **Strand**, once one of London's most fashionable streets. You can dine on

roast beef at **Simpson's**, opened in 1848, or take tea in the Thames Room of the **Savoy Hotel**. The hotel complex houses the **Savoy Theatre**, where Gilbert and Sullivan's operas were first staged.

From Strand, cut north up Southampton Street to reach one of London's most crowded tourist sites. Named after a convent whose fields occupied the site, ★★**Covent Garden ⓳** was for centuries the principal market for vegetables, fruit and flowers, and the workplace of Eliza Doolittle, the flower girl in George Bernard Shaw's *Pygmalion* who later burst into song as *My Fair Lady*. The market moved out in 1974 and, since the early 1980s, the area has seen a transformation that has become a blueprint for turning old commercial buildings into a characterful mall. Numerous restaurants and cafés, shops and showrooms occupy the old warehouses in the narrow streets and alleyways surrounding the market square. There is a good line in street entertainers.

The main piazza was originally laid out with colonnaded town houses designed by Inigo Jones around 1630, and inspired by the 16th-century Italian architect Andrea Palladio. A small market was established here as early as 1661. The terraces and arcades have long since disappeared, although the arcade on the north side has been re-cast. Many of the streets around Covent Garden have been cordoned off with pedestrian pathways.

The portico of **St Paul's**, the actors' church, used as a backdrop in *My Fair Lady* and also designed by Inigo Jones, dominates the western end of the square, on to which it turns its back. The vaults and grounds of this church are said to contain the remains of more famous people than any other church except Westminster Abbey, although the headstones have long been removed. An annual clowns' service is held here.

LONDON TRANSPORT MUSEUM

The old flower market, in the southeastern corner of the square, is now home to the ★★**London Transport Museum ⓴** (daily 10am–6pm, Fri 11am–6pm; fee for adults but free to accompanied

Star attractions
● **Covent Garden**
● **London Transport Museum**

Below: street entertainers in Covent Garden
Bottom: vintage buses in the London Transport Museum

Map on page 18

Neal's Yard
This tiny square off Shorts Gardens (north of Covent Garden's piazza) maintains the alternative traditions that helped save the area from the developers when the fruit and vegetable market moved south of the Thames in 1974. The brightly painted enclave has an acupuncturist, an apothecary, a bakery, natural food shops, designer outlets and cafés. Neal's Yard Dairy has a remarkable range of British cheeses.

children under 16). Its large collection of horse-drawn coaches, buses, trams, trains and rail carriages is the main attraction, but it also effectively traces the social history of modern London, whose growth was powered by transport, and deals intelligently with issues such as congestion and pollution. Facilities for children are especially good.

Next door to the transport museum, but entered from Russell Street, is the **Theatre Museum ㉑** (free), which contains portraits, costumes, stage sets and much memorabilia. The displays are a bit static and will appeal mostly to theatre fans, but costume workshops and makeup demonstrations are popular with both children and adults.

ROYAL OPERA HOUSE

In the northeast corner of Covent Garden is the ★**Royal Opera House ㉒**, refurbished just in time for the millennium at a cost of £120 million. Before the renovations, the politics behind the beautiful facade had been vicious and the backstage facilities cramped. After the reopening, the politics seemed more benign, and singers, dancers and musicians all had more space in which to rehearse and prepare for performances. Audiences at last benefited from air conditioning.

On the outside, Inigo Jones's piazza was completed, with colonnades running all the way round

The Royal Opera House

this corner of the piazza. Beneath them were two arcades and an entrance from the market square. For the first time the Royal Ballet Company now has a base at the Opera House, with six ballet studios and a performance studio seating 200. A further performance space, a 400-seat Studio Theatre, enables the two companies to give around 100 performances here a year. Ticket prices are high, but administrators continue to complain that opera in London in grossly underfunded.

Star attractions
● Trafalgar Square
● National Gallery
● National Portrait Gallery

TRAFALGAR SQUARE

Exit Covent Garden westwards along Long Acre, passing Stanford's, London's top map and guidebook store, and turn left down St Martin's Lane, home to several theatres. It leads into the monumental space of ★★**Trafalgar Square** ㉓. Designed by John Nash, it vividly reflects Britain at the height of its power, when its navy was invincible and it ruled more than a quarter of the planet. At the centre of the square is the 167-ft (50-metre) Corinthian column and 12-ft (3.6-metre) statue of Horatio Nelson, the admiral who defeated Napoleon Bonaparte at the Battle of Trafalgar in 1805. The four handsome lions (1847) are by Edwin Landseer. The square has long been the site of political demonstrations and New Year celebrations.

There is a rumour that the French crown jewels are buried beneath the square, placed there by Madame du Barry, mistress of Louis XV, when the site was part of the old royal mews.

Below: Trafalgar Square
Bottom: St Martin-in-the-Fields

MAJOR GALLERIES

On the square's north side is the imposing neo-classical facade of the ★★★**National Gallery** ㉔ and, to its right, the ★★★**National Portrait Gallery** ㉕ (*see Galleries, page 98*), both free.

The church on the east side of Trafalgar Square is **St Martin-in-the-Fields** ㉖, built in 1724 when there were fields here. Nell Gwynne, mistress of Charles II, is buried in this parish church, and the crypt houses a soup kitchen for the homeless.

Map on page 38

Where people meet: the Eros statue at Piccadilly Circus

3: Theatreland

Piccadilly Circus – Shaftesbury Avenue – Soho – Leicester Square – Charing Cross Road

★★**Piccadilly Circus** ㉗ is the heart of London's entertainments centre, the place where the first illuminated signs appeared in 1890. A few years later the statue of Eros, Greek god of love, was erected as the Angel of Charity in honour of the philanthropic Seventh Earl of Shaftesbury (1801–85) who drove the broad thoroughfare which bears his name through the squalid slums that had grown up to the northeast.

Adding to Piccadilly's bright lights are the re-furbished Criterion Theatre on the south side, and a former music hall, the London Pavilion, on the east. This now contains the high-tech **Trocadero Centre**, a massive shopping arcade with glass walkways, potted plants, waterfalls, a cinema and eateries such as Planet Hollywood and the Rainforest Café. There's also **Funland**, 'the world's biggest indoor family entertainment centre' (10am–midnight weekdays, 10am–1am weekends). There are five floors of video games, dodgems, ten-pin bowling, a sports bar, and a pool hall. **Shaftesbury Avenue** – a synonym for theatreland as 'Broadway' is in New York – is home to a string of mainstream theatres such as the Apollo and the Gielgud whose cramped bars and foyers are tolerated in the name of tradition.

SOHO

Shaftesbury Avenue cuts through **Soho**, an area long popular with immigrants. Flemish weavers, French Huguenots, Greeks, Italians, Belgians, Maltese, Swiss, Chinese and Russian Jews have sought refuge here. Their influence is still felt in the patisseries, delicatessens, restaurants and shops. Four hundred years ago Soho was an area of open fields, and its name is said to come from a hunting cry: 'So-ho, so-ho!'. Jazz clubs enhanced the area's bohemian reputation in the 1950s – Ronnie Scott's legendary club is still in

Frith Street – and artists such as Francis Bacon and Lucien Freud took advantage of the liberal alcohol licences in drinking dens such as the Colony Club in Dean Street. **Berwick Street** has a lively street market.

Today this cosmopolitan area is the heart of London's nightlife, with dozens of clubs, cabarets and strip clubs and, centred in Old Compton Street, the capital's main gay quarter. The local authority, Westminster, tries hard to keep the sleazy aspects under control.

Running parallel to the south side of Shaftesbury Avenue is Gerrard Street, heart of London's ★★**Chinatown** and the place to find authentic Chinese regional cuisine.

What saves Soho from being just a tourist trap is that several thousand people still live there, mostly in the kind of cramped conditions endured by Karl Marx in Dean Street in the 1850s. As a result, some local shops can still survive, though rising rents threaten to drive out both small retailers and residents.

The western, more residential part of Soho contains Brewer Street, which has a variety of specialist shops selling oddities such as vintage magazines, and **Carnaby Street** ㉘, once the epitome of Swinging London and now emerging from a period of total tackiness to become a centre for youth-oriented fashion.

Star attractions
● **Piccadilly Circus**
● **Chinatown**

Below: Soho's Chinatown
Bottom: Berwick Street market

Map on page 38

Below: some secondhand bookshops survive on Charing Cross Road
Bottom: Charlie Chaplin's statue in Leicester Square

LEICESTER SQUARE

To the south of Soho, **Leicester Square** ㉙, with several of London's largest cinemas, hosts movie premieres. Its pedestrian area and host of fast-food joints make it a natural meeting point for tourists and their natural companions – buskers, caricature artists and pickpockets. At the centre is the Shakespeare monument (1874) and a statue of comedian Charlie Chaplin, who was born in London. The **Notre Dame de France** church in Leicester Place (on the north side) has a mural by Jean Cocteau.

The Cranbourn Street exit from the square leads into ★**Charing Cross Road**, which has several more major theatres (such as the Palace, longtime home of *Les Misérables*, at Cambridge Circus) but is best known for its bookshops. High rents have driven out some of the maze-like secondhand bookshops immortalised in Helen Hanff's memoir *84 Charing Cross Road*, but some have survived alongside the big chains. Cecil Court, an alley at the southern end of the street, has some interesting specialist and antiquarian shops.

The flagship is ★**Foyles** ㉚, at the northern end, the biggest maze of all. Until recently it seemed that nobody, least of all its staff, could find their way around its 4 million books, but the death of its eccentric owner, Christina Foyle, has allowed a new management to introduce some order. Zwemmer's, nearby, has art and photography books.

4: Royal London

Piccadilly – Jermyn Street – St James's – Green Park – The Mall – Buckingham Palace

Piccadilly, named after the stiff collars ('pickadils') sold by a local trader to 18th-century dandies, is a fashionable street with many royal associations. The architecturally grand ★★**Royal Academy of Arts** ➌ *(see Galleries, page 99)* moved here in 1869. Artists belong to it, by election, and largely run it. Its Summer Exhibition, open to anyone whose work is judged to be good enough, is prominent on the social calendar.

Some of the capital's classiest small shops can be found in the area – some in Burlington Arcade, which runs down the west side of the Royal Academy, and others on **Jermyn Street**, which runs parallel to Piccadilly's south side. At 181 Piccadilly, ★**Fortnum and Mason** ➋, grocer to the Queen, is famous for its food hampers, food hall, and afternoon tea. The enterprise began with royal tastes in mind, as one of its founders, Charles Fortnum, was formerly a footman to George III.

Afternoon tea is also available close by at the **Ritz Hotel**, though it must be booked well in advance (tel: 7493 8181). The hotel, built in 1906 as London's first major steel-framed building, hasn't the cachet it once had, but its casino retains a touch of class. The elegant Louis XVI dining room overlooks Green Park.

At number 203 Piccadilly is **Waterstone's** flagship store, Europe's biggest bookshop. It used to be a department store and is worth a look for its classy 1930s interior.

ST JAMES'S

To the south of Piccadilly lies **St James's**, the epitome of aristocratic London. Along elegant **Pall Mall** ➌ exclusive clubs mingle with the grand homes of royalty, and their lofty book-lined rooms and elegant, picture-lined dining rooms and chandeliered drawing-rooms can be seen from the street. For the most part, the clubs

Blue plaques
Since the poet Lord Byron was thus commemorated in 1867, more than 600 circular blue plaques have been attached to buildings to denote where illustrious people once lived. Literary figures loom large, but those honoured also include Marx, Mozart, Gandhi, Benjamin Franklin, Charles de Gaulle and Jimi Hendrix.

Below: Royal Academy of Arts
Bottom: Fortnum and Mason

Map below

Queen's Walk

This path offers pedestrians a pleasant stroll through the 53-acre (21-hectare) Green Park from Green Park Underground station to Buckingham Palace. The less energetic can hire deckchairs at the Piccadilly end of the park. Some original gas lamps are still in place.

– mostly men-only – enjoy a reputation for dull food, excellent wine and snobbish company.

It is said that bishops and Fellows of the Royal Society join the Athenaeum, the foremost literary club, while diplomats, politicians and spies prefer Brooks', the Traveller's, Boodles or White's. The liberal Reform Club in Pall Mall is where Phileas Fogg wagered he could travel *Around the World in 80 Days* in Jules Verne's 1873 novel.

GREEN PARK

Also on the south side of Piccadilly is **Green Park**, a favourite spot for 18th-century duels and the setting for the 1749 pyrotechnic display that

premiered Handel's *Music for the Royal Fireworks*. The Queen's Walk, running along the east side, is a pleasant escape from the traffic and leads past the side of ★**Spencer House** (27 St James's Place, tel: 7499 8620; Sundays only except Jan & Aug, 10.30am–5.30pm). One of London's earliest examples of neoclassical architecture, this private palace was built in 1756–66 for the Spencer family (of which Diana, Princess of Wales, was the most celebrated recent member) and has been renovated to its late 18th-century appearance. It provides both a classical showcase and, with eight state rooms, a sumptuous setting for receptions.

To the south, at the end of Pall Mall, are two other royal residences, the red-brick ★**St James's Palace**, built by Henry VIII in the style of Hampton Court, and, behind it, **Clarence House**, the residence of Queen Elizabeth the Queen Mother until her death in 2002. Neither is open to the public, but the chief relic of St James's Palace, the gatehouse, or clock tower, a fine piece of Tudor architecture, is best viewed from Pall Mall.

Marlborough Road leads down to **The Mall**, a wide throroughfare leading from Buckingham Palace to Trafalgar Square, laid out by Charles II as a second course for the popular French game of *paille maille*, a kind of croquet, when the one in Pall Mall became too rowdy. In front of the palace is the **Queen Victoria Memorial 34**, built in 1901 and encompassing symbolic figures which glorify the achievements of the British Empire and its builders.

BUCKINGHAM PALACE

★★**Buckingham Palace 35** has been the main London home of the royal family since Queen Victoria moved here in 1837. Her uncle, George IV, had employed John Nash to enlarge the building, which was constructed in the 17th century for a Duke of Buckingham. Nash added two wings, later enclosed in a quadrangle, and its main facade was designed by Aston Webb in 1913.

The State Rooms are open to the public for a few weeks in August/September when the Queen

Star attraction
● **Buckingham Palace**

Below: St James's Palace
Bottom: the Duke of Wellington memorial on the Mall

Map
on page
38

Below: a Horse Guard
Bottom: Buckingham Palace

is away (tel: 7321 2233, recorded info: 7799 2331; www.the-royal-collection.org.uk). These include the Dining Room, Music Room, White Drawing Room and Throne Room, where there are paintings by Vermeer, Rubens and Rembrandt.

The tour also allows a glimpse of the 40-acre (16-hectare) Palace Gardens where the celebrated garden parties are held; guests are invited because of some worthy contribution made to the nation, but few of the 8,000 people a year get to shake the Queen's hand.

The Queen and the Duke of Edinburgh occupy about 12 of the palace's 650 rooms, on the first floor of the north wing, overlooking Green Park. If the Queen is in residence, the royal standard flies from the centre flagpole. On great occasions the family appears on the first-floor balcony to wave to the crowds.

Most of the everyday crowds come to see the Changing of the Guard at 11.30am (alternate mornings in winter) outside the palace. The New Guard, which marches up from Wellington Barracks, meets the Old Guard in the forecourt of the palace and they exchange symbolic keys to the accompaniment of regimental music. The Irish

Guards are distinctive for their bearskin hats (now made from synthetic materials). Behind the scenes are more sophisticated protection measures: there is a large nuclear shelter underneath the palace.

The Queen has one of the greatest private art collections in the world – around 9,000 works, including an exceptional collection of Leonardo da Vinci drawings – and a selection of her paintings is on show in the ★★**Queen's Gallery** ㊱ (Buckingham Palace Road, tel: 7839 1377; daily 10am–5.30pm; fee). It is rich in royal portraits, notably by Holbein and Van Dyck.

ROYAL TRANSPORT

The adjoining ★★**Royal Mews** ㊲ (tel: 7839 1377; Aug–Sept Mon–Thurs 10.30am–4.30pm; Oct–July Mon–Thurs noon–4pm; fee) contain royal vehicles, from coaches to Rolls-Royces. The spotless stables accommodate as many as 30 horses and the Gold State Coach, built for George III in 1762, is kept here. The mews is a charming place, tucked away to the side of Buckingham Palace near Buckingham Gate. Less formal than the palace and less touristy than the Changing of the Guard, it provides an insight into the workings of the Royal Household, full of quiet details such as the weight of a coachman's red-and-gold livery (16 lbs/7 kg) and the news that on State occasions everyone rises at 5am.

The nearest Tube is Victoria, at the end of Buckingham Palace Road, but on a fine day you might wish to stroll into ★**St James's Park** ㊳, on the south side of the Mall. This formal arrrangement of lakes and flora is one of the most delightful in London. Formerly the grounds of St James's Palace, it was created by John Nash and the great 18th-century landscape gardener 'Capability' Brown, but was later wrecked in a peace celebration gala at the end of the Napoleonic Wars in 1814. It has always had a collection of ducks and water fowl, including black swans, and there have long been pelicans in residence here. They are fed every day at 3pm. Another entertainment is the lunchtime concerts played in the bandstand. In summer, deckchairs can be hired.

Star attractions
● **The Queen's Gallery**
● **Royal Mews**

Guards Museum
Those intrigued by the Changing of the Guard at Buckingham Palace can find out more about the five Foot Guards regiments (Coldstream, Grenadier, Scots, Irish and Welsh) at this museum at the west end of Wellington Barracks on Birdcage Walk. It tries hard to be a social history in uniform, telling the stories of the soldiers from all classes of society. Much of the collection is displayed at child's-eye level.

St James's Park, looking towards the London Eye on the other side of the Thames

Map on page 38

5: Shopper's London

Piccadilly – Regent Street – Oxford Street – New Bond Street – Tottenham Court Road

Retail temples: Liberty, Regent Street (below) and Selfridges, Oxford Street (bottom)

From the massive Tower Records store at Piccadilly Circus, **Regent Street** begins its graceful sweep north. It was designed by the architect John Nash as a ceremonial route linking Carlton House, the long-demolished Prince Regent's residence at Piccadilly, to the green expanse of Regent's Park, but the main ceremony today is running gold credit cards through the tills of of Next, Gap, Laura Ashley, Aquascutum, Burberry, Jaeger and Austin Reed. At number 68 is the **Café Royal**, used by such belle époque figures as George Bernard Shaw, Oscar Wilde, James Whistler and Aubrey Beardsley.

At number 214 the grand Arts and Crafts champion, ★**Liberty** ㊴, is housed in an imposing Tudor-style building constructed using the timber of two ships. Since it was founded in 1875 by a draper's son, Arthur Lasenby Liberty, this popular store has been renowned for its style and elegance. Nowadays it is home to one of London's most desirable collections of furniture, fabrics (look out for the famous paisley patterns), designer fashion, accessories and toiletries, and it's worth a visit if only for a peek inside the magnificent building.

There's a Disney Store at numbers 140–144,

but it is overshadowed at numbers 188–196 by
★**Hamley's** ④⓪, a celebrated toyshop with seven
floors filled with every imaginable toy from board
games to hi-tech robots. The store is like a fair-
ground, with a haunted staircase and interactive
play-stations.

OXFORD STREET

At Oxford Circus, Regent Street intersects with
Oxford Street, London's most crowded shopping
thoroughfare. Ahead, Upper Regent Street mostly
contains imposing but nondescript office buildings.
More imposing than most is **Broadcasting House**,
headquarters of the BBC, in Portland Place, with
its Eric Gill sculpture showing Shakespeare's Pros-
pero sending Ariel, the symbol of broadcasting, out
into the world. To cope with the BBC's growth, the
1932 building is being ambitiously extended.

Oxford Street – named after the Earl of Oxford,
who owned land locally – was begun in the
1760s, though a road to the west had existed here
since Roman times. The classier half is to the
west of Oxford Circus and is dominated by large
department stores – although there are still a fair
number of kitsch stalls selling Union Jack-
branded T-shirts.

Behind the Ionic columns of ★**Selfridges** ④①,
founded by Wisconsin businessman Henry Gordon Selfridge in 1907, is a shopping experience
not to be missed. All this season's cutting-edge
fashion labels are here, plus everything from pots
and pans to refrigerators plus an extravagantly
stocked Food Hall. **John Lewis**, another department store, stresses value-for-money, selling fashion and household essentials under the motto
'never knowingly undersold'.

At the west end of Oxford Street is **Marble
Arch**, erected in 1827 in front of Buckingham
Palace and moved here in 1851 when it proved
too narrow for the State coaches to pass through.
The traffic island in which it now resides was
the site of Tyburn Tree, a triangular gallows on
which as many as 50,000 people were publicly
hanged between 1571 and 1759.

The Wallace Collection
Slightly north of Oxford Street, in an elegant town-
house on Manchester Square, is the Wallace Collection *(see page 100)*, one of London's lesser-known galleries. The collection is comprised mostly of 18th-century French paint-
ings, porcelain and furniture and was bequeathed to the nation in 1897. There's a lovely café here and concerts are often held in the gallery over Sunday breakfast.

Below: teddies at Hamley's
Bottom: grandeur at Selfridges

Map on page 38

Father of Electricity
Part of the Royal Institution at 21 Albemarle Street is the **Michael Faraday Laboratory & Museum** (Mon–Fri 9am–5pm). It celebrates the career of Faraday (1791–1867), a blacksmith's son from Surrey often described as the father of electricity. The one-room museum reconstructs his laboratory, where he discovered the principles that led to the electric motor, the transformer and the generator.

Guarding fragile merchandise

MAYFAIR

Although Top Shop at Oxford Circus pulls in hordes of fashion-aware, budget-conscious shoppers with its affordable catwalk copies, the real fashionistas head for **Bond Street**, which runs from Oxford Street towards Piccadilly. The area, known as **Mayfair**, has been an icon of wealth and power since the early 18th century, when it was laid out by the Grosvenor family, dukes of Westminster. Here are London's most exclusive couturiers and designer boutiques, jewellery shops, antique stores and art galleries. Think of a prestige name, from Armani to Versace, from Mulberry's handbags to Church's English shoes, and it's likely to be here.

The headquarters of **Sotheby's** ❷, the auctioneers founded in 1744 and now American-owned, is at No. 34. This is where world record prices for art works are notched up, but not every sale is for millionaires. Admission is free, as long as you look reasonably presentable.

Upmarker stores such as Asprey and Fenwick's are part of Bond Street's fabric. Art galleries proliferate here and in adjacent Bruton Street, but their focal point is **Cork Street** ❸, parallel to Bond Street to the east, with such prestigious premises as Waddington's and the Cork Street Gallery, where Britain's top artists are represented and where museum-quality

works are for sale. Just beyond is **Savile Row** ⓐ, home of gentlemen's outfitters, where even 'off-the-peg' items are highly priced.

A friendly statue of General Eisenhower and Winston Churchill having a chat on a bench in Bond Street is a sign of the interest Americans have always had in Mayfair. In 1785 John Adams, the first United States minister to Britain and later the nation's president, took up residence at **9 Grosvenor Square**. Today the square is dominated by the heavily guarded **American Embassy** ⓑ, with its defensive 'moat' and enormous eagle. The cost of the statue of Franklin D. Roosevelt in the gardens was met by grateful British citizens after World War II.

Fans of Handel's *Messiah* may wish to check out **Handel House Museum** ⓒ (Tues–Sat) at 25 Brook Street, the house where the composer lived from 1723 until his death in 1759. The Georgian interiors have been restored, Handel memorabilia is being assembled and live music is sometimes played on one of two harpsichords.

Next door, at number 23, a blue plaque on the wall confirms that a very different musician, rock star Jimi Hendrix, lived here in 1968.

Also in Brook Street is **Claridge's**, a luxury hotel favoured by visiting movie stars.

TOTTENHAM COURT ROAD

The half of Oxford Street to the east of Oxford Circus contains its fair share of large shops, from Marks & Spencer to a Virgin Megastore, but it is less upmarket than the other half. It leads to the junction of Charing Cross Road, famed for its bookshops (*see page 36*) and **Tottenham Court Road**. Although the latter, with its heavy traffic and its preponderance of tacky shop signage, has little to offer in the way of charm, the northern end of the street is one of the best areas for top-end home furnishings (at stores such as Heal's and Habitat), and the southern end is awash with cut-price hi-fi and computer stores, each selling much the same stock but giving a little scope for bargaining.

Below: the American Embassy
Centre: Handel House Museum
Bottom: a familiar sight on Tottenham Court Road

Map below

6: Knightsbridge & Kensington

Hyde Park Corner – Knightsbridge – South Kensington – Kensington High Street

---

A hardy tradition
At 9am each Christmas Day, swimmers dive into the Serpentine lake to compete for the Peter Pan Cup, first presented by children's author J.M. Barrie. The temperature is usually just above freezing, but sometimes the ice must be broken.

When combined with the adjacent Kensington Gardens, ★★**Hyde Park** is London's biggest public park (340 acres/138 hectares). Henry VIII closed off the area in 1536, stocking it with deer, but Charles I opened it up to the people in 1635.

There are many paths across the park: the South Carriage Drive follows the southern edge of the park from the entrance as far as Alexandra Gate; another path heads north alongside Park Lane to the northeast entrance by Marble Arch. More or less parallel to South Carriage Drive is the

horse promenade, Rotten Row or *route du roi* (the king's path), which was once taken by the king on his way to the royal hunting grounds and is still used by well-heeled riders and their mounts.

Follow the middle path northeast to the **Serpentine** ㊼, a long, narrow lake which is a haven for wildfowl and a popular spot for boating, swimming and fishing. A bridge offers a splendid view over the park and the **Serpentine Gallery** (tel: 7298 1515), a former tea-house, is now a hip white space hosting important exhibitions of modern and contemporary art. To the west of the bridge is a statue of J.M. Barrie's **Peter Pan**.

To leave the park, make for the northeast corner and **Speakers' Corner** ㊽, where soapbox orators and hecklers exercise their right to free speech, mostly on Sunday afternoons. This was the location of the ancient Tyburn gallows, where the condemned were allowed to speak freely before being executed. To the north, the huge triumphal **Marble Arch** (1828) was planned as the royal entrance to Buckingham Palace, but the architect forgot to measure the width of the carriages and the middle arch was too narrow.

Park Lane, home to expensive showrooms, apartments and hotels, leads to Hyde Park Corner, where the triumphal sculpture of a four-horsepower chariot is stranded in the middle of a traffic island atop **Constitution Arch** ㊾. Built to commemorate the Duke of Wellington's beating Napoleon at Waterloo in 1815 and popularly known as Wellington Arch, it contains three floors of historical exhibits and a viewing balcony. Facing it is the duke's home, **Apsley House**. Designed by Robert Adam, it is now partly the residence of the duke's descendants and partly the ★**Wellington Museum** (Tues–Sun 11am–4.30pm; fee). The collection of paintings include Velazquez and Caravaggio, and the 4,000 other objects include silverware, gold daggers and elaborate candelabra.

To the south lies Belgravia, one of London's most expensive residential areas and to the west is **Knightsbridge**, with shops well suited to the residents. Chief among these, on Brompton Road, is ★**Harrods**, London's most famous department

Star attraction
● **Hyde Park**

Below: these gates into Hyde Park from Park Lane have not received universal praise
Bottom: Harrods

Map on page 46

👁 **A magnet for musicians**
More than 600 instruments dating from the 15th century to the present day are on display in the **Royal College of Music Museum of Instruments** (Prince Consort Road, SW7, tel: 7589 3643, Wed 2–4.30pm during term time). Exhibits include a clavicytherium from south Germany (*circa* 1480), the earliest known surviving stringed keyboard instrument and a forerunner of today's pianos.

store. The business was founded by a grocer, Henry Charles Harrod, in 1849, although the present building dates from 1905. The business was bought in 1983 by the Egyptian Al-Fayed family. It's worth visiting the elegant food hall, decorated with art nouveau tiles and mosaics.

Continuing down the Cromwell Road, the main route to the M4 and Heathrow airport, takes you past **Brompton Oratory** ➎. This Roman Catholic church, with its 190-ft (66-metre) dome, was built between 1854 and 1884 in the Italian baroque style and contains great Carrara marble statues of the apostles, which once graced the cathedral at Siena. There are also noteworthy mosaics.

To the west lie a trio of fabulous (and free) museums, the ★★★**Victoria and Albert Museum**, the ★★★**Natural History Museum** and the ★★★**Science Museum** (*see pages 50–54*). The inspiration behind this concentration of culture was Prince Albert, consort of Queen Victoria, a moving spirit behind the 1851 Great Exhibition of Industry of All Nations. He argued that a permanent exhibition of applied arts would educate British manufacturers in the relationship between fine art and design, and the profits from the Great Exhibition were used to buy a block of land.

Albert has more personal memorials on **Kensington Gore**, the extension of Knisghtsbridge that runs to the south of Hyde Park. The ★**Royal**

The Albert Memorial

Albert Hall ❺ (1870), an ornate circular building with a capacity of 8,000, measures 272ft by 238ft (83 by 73 metres), the glass and iron dome is 135ft (41 metres) high internally and the 150-ton organ has 10,000 pipes. The frieze around the outside illustrates 'The Triumph of Arts and Sciences'. Events at the hall range from tennis and boxing to classical and rock concerts. Every July the BBC stages the **Henry Wood Promenade Concerts**, mixing new music with old favourites.

Across the road in Kensington Gardens is the apogee of the Albert cult, the **Albert Memorial ❺** designed by Sir George Gilbert Scott. Its gilded glory – or gaudy vulgarity, depending on taste – depicts the prince as a great god or philosopher, clutching in his right hand the catalogue of the Great Exhibition which he masterminded. Marking the corners of the monument are symbols for the spread of the British Empire: a camel for Africa, a bull bison for America, an elephant for Asia and a cow for Europe (Australia, then the Empire's dumping ground for convicts, isn't mentioned).

Nearby on Kensington Gore are the **Royal College of Art**, where Henry Moore and David Hockney studied, and the **Royal Geographical Society**, which holds occasional exhibitions.

KENSINGTON HIGH STREET

Kensington Gore runs into Kensington High Street, a noted shopping area. Diana, Princess of Wales, used to live in ★★**Kensington Palace ❺**, the seat of monarchs until 1760, and some minor royals still have apartments here. The ornate State Apartments can be visited (Mar–Oct 10am–6pm, Nov–Feb 10am–5pm). The richly decorated drawing rooms and bedrooms contain many of their original furnishings, and there are displays of ceremonial dresses and uniforms, and some fine paintings from the Royal Collection. The sunken gardens and classical Orangery (now a café) are worth a visit.

It's also worth visiting **Leighton House** (12 Holland Park Road, Mon–Sat 11am–5.30pm), which the Victorian aesthete Lord Frederic Leighton (1830–96) filled with oil paintings and Arab decor.

Star attraction
● **Kensington Palace**

Below: Royal Albert Hall
Bottom: the Royal Ceremonial Dress Collection is on display at Kensington Palace

Map on page 46

A Gothic extravaganza
The Natural History Museum was designed in 1881 by Alfred Waterhouse in the Gothic Romanesque style. It was the first building in Britain to be faced entirely in terracotta, a cheap but versatile material that could be easily cleaned and came in lovely shades of buff and pale-blue. With Romanesque arches, Gothic pinnacles, stained-glass windows and nave-like Central Hall, it's more like a cathedral than a museum, a similarity intended by Professor Richard Owen, its first director. He felt the building should celebrate God's creation. The result is a joy. Terracotta monkeys scramble up pillars; cranes, hares and lizards peep through foliage; songbirds are everywhere.

Below: dinosaurs on display

7: South Kensington's Museums

Not only are these three astonishing collections among the best in the world, they are also free.

★★★ NATURAL HISTORY MUSEUM ❺❹

Cromwell Road, SW7. Tel: 7942 5000.
www.nhm.ac.uk; *10am (Sun 11am)–5.50pm; free*
If any of London's museums encapsulates the Victorians' quest for knowledge and passion for sifting and cataloguing data, it's this one, with its collection of 75 million plants, animals, fossils, rocks and minerals. Its collection is growing by 50,000 new specimens a year, and it has impressive high-tech exhibits such as animatronic dinosaurs and a simulated earthquake.

In spite of its vast size, the layout is easy to master. It divides between the 'Life' galleries, starting from Cromwell Road, and the 'Earth' galleries, beginning from Exhibition Road. Waterhouse Way connects the two.

THE LIFE GALLERIES

Dinosaurs (21). Many visitors make a bee-line for the robotic dinosaurs, especially the full-scale T-Rex. Responsive to human movement, the roaring, life-like model twists and turns.
Human Biology (22). Examining the workings behind every part of the human body, from

hormones to genes, this section is packed with interactive exhibits. More on genetics and the possibilities of genetic engineering can be found in the exhibition on Darwin and the Origin of Species (105) on the first floor.

Mammals (23 and 24). As well as displaying an astonishing array of taxidermy, these galleries contain sobering statistics on the rate at which species are becoming extinct.

Fish and Amphibians (12). This gallery highlights many fascinating species, including fish that live between the sea's twilight zone at 1,300 ft (400 metres) and total darkness at 3,300ft (1,000 metres); some generate their own light.

Waterhouse Way. The walls of this central corridor are lined with impressive marine fossils.

Creepy Crawlies (33). This section is a mine of astonishing and sometimes flesh-crawling facts. You can sit in a life-size model of a termite mound, or watch a colony of leaf-cutter ants.

THE EARTH GALLERIES

A central escalator transports visitors into a gigantic rotating globe. At the top, **Restless Surface (62)** includes imaginative coverage of earthquakes and volcanoes. **From the Beginning (63)** relates the story of the universe from the time of the big bang 15,000 million years ago to the end of the solar system, predicted 5,000 million years from now. **Earth's Treasury (64)** displays rocks, gems and minerals.

★★★ SCIENCE MUSEUM ⑤⑤

Exhibition Road, SW7. Tel: 0870-870 4771. www.sciencemuseum.org.uk; *10am–6pm; free*
With more than 10,000 exhibits plus an IMAX theatre, this museum could occupy a full day. You can walk between the main wing, dating to 1928, and the Wellcome Wing, opened in 2000, at five of the museum's seven levels, but the ambience of the wings is quite different and it's more satisfying to explore one wing at a time.

Main Wing: Ground Floor. This is the Science Museum at its spectacular best. The Power Hall is

Star Attractions
● **Natural History Museum**
● **Science Museum**

> **The Darwin Centre**
> Situated next to the NHM, in Queen's Gate, this building is both a top-class centre for scientific study and a public resource. 'Meet the Scientists' sessions are planned. Over 22 million specimens have already been moved here and 28 million insects, 6 million plants and 25,000 jars of plankton are due to join them.

Below: the Earth Galleries

Map on page 46

Below: reconstruction of the 1969 lunar landing
Bottom: the Making of the Modern World gallery

dominated by a massive 1903 mill engine which worked 1,700 looms in Burnley until 1970 and still rotates with great elegance. An impressive variety of engines, some models but many full-size, trace the development of steam power from the early 18th century. The Exploration of Space gallery's big attraction is a replica of the Apollo 11 lunar excursion module. Making the Modern World includes the world's oldest surviving steam locomotive, the coal-hauling Puffing Billy (*circa* 1815), Stephenson's pioneering *Rocket* passenger locomotive (1829), a Ford Model T (1916), and a Lockheed Electra airliner (1935).

First Floor. Galleries include materials, tele-communications, gas, agriculture, surveying, time measurement, food and weather.

Second Floor. Galleries cover chemistry, printing and papermaking, weighing and measuring, lighting, nuclear physics and power, computing and mathematics, ships, marine engineering and diving.

Third floor. Galleries cover heat and temperature, geophysics and oceanography, optics, photography and cinematography, health, flight and broadcasting. Dominating this floor is the magnificent Flight Gallery, with exhibits ranging from a seaplane to a Spitfire, from hot-air balloons to helicopters. The 1919 Vickers Vimy in which Alcock & Brown made the first non-stop transatlantic flight is here.

Fourth and Fifth Floors. These cover medicine and veterinary history, with exhibits ranging from early surgical instruments to open-heart surgery.

Basement. The Garden is a play area for children aged 3–6, and Things is a hands-on 'how do things work?' gallery for 7–11-year-olds. Also here is The Secret Life of the Home, a collection of domestic appliances and gadgets that provoke nostalgia in adults and disbelief in children.

The Wellcome Wing. Providing further interest for children, Launch Pad, in the Wellcome Wing section of the basement, is a spacious interactive gallery with an emphasis on learning about science and technology. The remaining floors concentrate on digital technology, biomedical science and information technology. An IMAX film theatre conjures up dinosaurs or outer space on a screen 65ft (20 metres) wide. Digitopolis shows how new technology may change our lives.

★★★ VICTORIA AND ALBERT MUSUEM ⑤⑥

Cromwell Road, SW7. Tel: 7942 2000.
www.vam.ac.uk; *10am–5.45pm (Wed 10pm); free*
With 5 million objects and almost 8 miles (13 km) of galleries, this museum (founded in 1852) is colossal. One minute one can be admiring Raphael's cartoons for the Sistine Chapel tapestries, and the next examining E.H. Shepard's illustrations for Winnie-the-Pooh. Big spending is planned to make the collections more accessible.

THE HIGHLIGHTS

Europe and America 1800–1900. This includes pieces shown at the Great Exhibition of 1851. The massive bookcases and armoires in extravagant Gothic Revival style are finely crafted.

The Sculpture Courts. These contain British and European neoclassical works from the late 18th and early 19th centuries.

Raphael Cartoons (1515–16). These highly finished preparatory drawings were templates for tapestries in the Sistine Chapel.

Dress. The history of male and female costume.

The Asian and Islamic Collections focus on

Star Attraction
● **Victoria and Albert Museum**

Albert's big idea
Eager to educate British manufacturers in the relationship between fine art and design, Queen Victoria's husband, Prince Albert, a moving spirit behind the 1851 Great Exhibition, backed the purchase of a block of land on which the South Kensington Museum of Science and Art opened in 1857. The present imposing building, when completed in 1909, was renamed the Victoria and Albert Museum.

Main entrance, the Victoria and Albert Museum

Map on page 46

The Ceramic Staircase
This magnificent creation, completed in 1869, symbolises the relationship between art and science. Its twin circular ceilings show the Greek gods of agriculture, commerce, industry and the arts.

Below: Vivienne Westwood's platform shoes (1993)
Bottom: 17th-century display in the British Galleries

Indian Art, Arts of the Islamic World, and China, Japan, Southest Asia and Korea.

Plaster Casts and Fakes & Forgeries. Copies of vast monuments, tombs, pillars, friezes and effigies include Michelangelo's *David*.

The Italian Collection contains outstanding Renaissance pieces, concentrated in Rooms 12–20. Room 16 contains the finest collection of work by Donatello (1386–1466) outside Italy.

The Upper Levels. Many of these galleries focus on materials or techniques, such as silver, iron-work, stained glass, ceramics and textiles.

The British Galleries, documenting British taste, are as much about the movement of ideas as the ideas themselves. Among the many highlights is the fabulous late 16th-century Great Bed of Ware, a four-poster of such enormous proportions that it was already a tourist attraction in 1596. Antonio Canova's *The Three Graces* (1814) is here too.

The Hereford Screen, a choir screen of cast iron and brass, is studded with semi-precious stones.

Glass, Jewellery, Silver and Ceramics. The size of the jewellery collection is overwhelming. Ceramics (European and British porcelain, pottery, tiles, and Far Eastern ceramics) is said to be the largest in the world.

The Henry Cole Wing has drawings, paintings and photographs. Here also is the Frank Lloyd Wright Room, transplanted from Pittsburgh.

8: Chelsea

Sloane Square – King's Road – Cheyne Walk

The traffic-congested **Sloane Square ⑤⑦** combines culture with commerce. On one side is the Royal Court Theatre, whose radical tradition embraces George Bernard Shaw's plays in the first years of the 20th century and John Osborne's in the 1960s. On the opposite side is the no-nonsense Peter Jones department store, founded by a Welsh draper's assistant in 1877.

Leading off the square is the **King's Road**, which Charles II (1660–85) designated his private route linking St James's Court to Hampton Palace and which was the epicentre of Swinging London in the 1960s and of the punk movement in the 1970s. Today the King's Road is a notable destination for interior designers wanting to select the best in wallpaper and fabric design and also has a profusion of soft furnishing shops such as Heal's. Opposite Heal's, the Chelsea Old Town Hall holds frequent crafts and antiques fairs and contains a register office favoured by celebrities keen to tie the knot.

Below: King's Road
Bottom: looking for antiques

BOOKS AND GARDENS

Just after the town hall, turn left down Oakley Street, right into Upper Cheyne Row and left into Cheyne Row, where ★ **Carlyle's House ⑤⑧** (Wed–Sun Apr–Oct, 11am–5pm; fee) is at number 24. The appeal of this narrow house is that it has been preserved pretty much as it looked when the dour Scottish essayist Thomas Carlyle died in 1881. The ground-floor parlour has its piano (on which Chopin once played), the kitchen has a dresser with a shelf that served as the maid's bed, the first-floor library contains Carlyle's books, and the attic study, lit by a skylight, is where he set down his thoughts on such subjects as Chartism, the French Revolution, and the Negro Question. There's a strong sense of how lives were lived in the house.

At this point you can walk across Albert Bridge to visit **Battersea Park ⑤⑨**, which includes Henry

Map on page 46

Fulham Palace
At the far end of New King's Road, near Putney Bridge, is the manor where the Bishops of London, once fabulously wealthy, lived for a thousand years until 1973. A two-room museum in the present somewhat characterless 16th-century palace can be visited (Mar–Oct Wed–Sun 2–5pm, Nov–Feb Thur–Sun 1–4pm; fee), but the real attraction is a stroll in the fine gardens, which introduced species such as magnolia to Britain.

Moore sculptures, sub-tropical gardens, a lake and a riverside **Buddhist Peace Pagoda** built in 1985. Otherwise, you can proceed to the east along the riverside Cheyne Walk to the ★ **Chelsea Physic Garden ⑩** (entrance at 66 Royal Hospital Road, Wed noon–5pm, Sun 2–6pm, Apr–Oct only; fee). This 'secret garden' dedicated to rare and medicinal plants was established in 1673 and contains an eccentric collection of trees and herbs, including poisonous specimens such as mandrake and deadly nightshade.

Further along Royal Hospital Road are the **National Army Museum** and the ★ **Royal Hospital ⑪**. The museum (10am–5.30pm; free), housed in a forbidding concrete block, charts the army's campaigns from the Middle Ages to modern times, from swords to heat-seeking missiles. There's a lot to see: medals and topographical models, Gainsborough portraits and computer-aided simulations. The hospital (Mon–Sat 10am–noon, Sun 2–4pm; free), a magnificent building created by Sir Christopher Wren in 1692, is home to the Chelsea Pensioners, uniformed war veterans who live here. A tour gives you the chance to chat to them.

Each year in the last week of May the Royal Horticultural Society holds the prestigious Chelsea Flower Show in the hospital's grounds. The public are admitted on the Thursday and Friday.

The Buddhist Peace Pagoda in Battersea Park

9: Marylebone & Bloomsbury

Baker Street – Marylebone Road – Regent's Park – Euston Road – Coram Fields

Map on page 58

Star attraction
● London Zoo

North of Oxford Street is the capital's intellectual area, home to London University, the British Museum and the former Bloomsbury literary set. Regent's Park and London Zoo provide breathing space.

The residential area of **Marylebone** (pronounced *mar-luh-bun*) is largely 18th-century and parts of Marylebone High Street and Marylebone Lane retain a village atmosphere, with small shops and pubs catering to the apartment blocks' inhabitants. Many of London's top doctors and dentists have their surgeries around Harley Street and Wimpole Street. The Art Nouveau ★ **Wigmore Hall** ② in Wigmore Street (parallel with Oxford Street) is a notable venue for lunchtime concerts and chamber music.

Below: the sitting room in the Sherlock Holmes Museum
Bottom: falconry, London Zoo

BAKER STREET

Baker Street Underground station is the gateway to several local attractions. At 221B Baker Street is the ★ **Sherlock Holmes Museum** ③ (9.30am–6.30pm; fee), paying tribute to fiction's greatest sleuth by creating an imaginative evocation of a Victorian apartment, complete with a 'maid' who will answer questions. A familiarity with Sir Arthur Conan Doyle's stories helps but isn't essential.

Continuing along Baker Street brings you to ★ **Regent's Park** ④, an elegant 470-acre (190-hectare) space surrounded by John Nash's handsome Regency terraces. The gardens are formally planted, and there's an Open Air Theatre where Shakespeare's plays are staged in summer. The boating lake is a tranquil spot, and Regent's Canal runs through the north of the park.

A big attraction is ★★ **London Zoo** ⑤, which has more than 8,000 animals and puts an emphasis on breeding programmes for endangered species. The penguin pool by the Russian architect Berthold Lubetkin and the aviary by Lord Snowdon are of architectural interest. The animals can be handled in the children's enclosure.

Below: Madame Tussaud's, the world's most popular waxworks

The Web of Life Exhibition, a glass pavilion, celebrates the variety of biological diversity.

To the northwest of the park is **Lord's Cricket Ground** ⑥⑥, the ancestral home of cricket. To visit the ground and its memorabilia-packed museum, you have to take a 90-minute tour, daily except on important match days at 10am (summer only), noon and 2pm (tel: 7432 1033).

MADAME TUSSAUD'S

The biggest attraction close to Baker Street Underground station is ★★**Madame Tussaud's** ⑥⑦ (Jul–Sept 9am–5.30pm, Oct–Jun 10am–5.30pm; fee), on Marylebone Road, where up to 7,000 people a day come to gaze at mute, immobile effigies with glass-fibre bodies and wax heads. A key ingredient in the waxworks' success is that models are not roped off or protected by glass cases. You can stroll right up to them, berate a dictator or put your arm around a Hollywood idol.

The museum was founded in 1835 by Marie Tussaud, who had prepared death masks of famous victims of the guillotine during the French

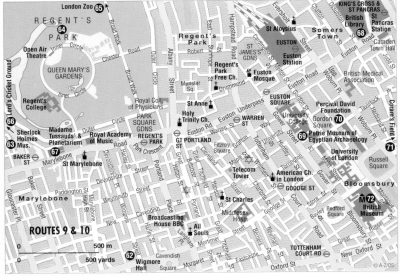

Revolution. Those gory beginnings are echoed in the waxworks' Chamber of Horrors, which contains the blade that sliced off Marie Antoinette's head and re-creates various tableaux of torture.

An attraction of Tussaud's has always been passing judgement on the quality of the likenesses, which varies from the barely recognisable to the astonishingly realistic. Audio-animatronics has breathed new life into some figures in a 'ride' through historical London. To avoid queues, buy timed tickets in advance.

Next door is the **London Planetarium**, where 20-minute projections onto the interior of the large dome explain the cosmos in a fairly basic way. It's worthy enough but can seem slow to children used to the pace of *Star Wars* movies.

BLOOMSBURY

Marylebone Road leads into Euston Road, to the south of which lies literary Bloomsbury, where blue plaques mark the one-time residences of luminaries such as Virginia Woolf and Lytton Strachey. Appropriately, the ★★**British Library** ❻❽ is on Euston Road, near the ornate St Pancras railway station. Galleries display some of the library's treasures, ranging from a 3rd-century biblical manuscript to original copies of Beatles lyrics.

The area's highlight is the ★★★**British Museum** (*see following pages*). At the other end of the scale, the two-room **Petrie Museum of Egyptian Archaeology** ❻❾ (University College, Malet Place, Tues–Fri 1–5pm, Sat 10am–1pm; free) has a specialist collection of Egyptian antiquities. At 15 Gordon Square, the ★**Percival David Foundation** ❼⓿ (Mon–Fri 10.30am–5pm; free) has one of the world's finest collections of Chinese ceramics.

Confirmed fans of Charles Dickens should visit 48 Doughty Street, where the novelist lived from 1837 to 1839. Now the ★**Dickens House Museum** (Mon–Sat 10am–5pm; fee), it contains a collection of his letters, furniture and possessions.

Coram Fields ❼❶, a children's adventure playground, includes sports pitches and a petting zoo. Unaccompanied adults may be refused admission.

Star attractions
● Madame Tussaud's
● British Library
● British Museum

Below: Kylie Minogue captured in wax at Madame Tussaud's
Bottom: Britain's book treasury

Plan on page 64

10: The British Museum

This world-class institution **72** on Great Russell Street contains 6½ million objects, ranging from prehistoric pots to a Cona coffee machine. Devote just 60 seconds to each one and you'd be there, without sleep or meal breaks, for more than 12 years. Even though only 50,000 objects are on display at any given time, this is not a place to 'do' in a couple of hours. It is a treasure house that caters for scholars as well as tourists and, as the scholars do, it is best to concentrate initially on what interests you most. A tour of the highlights *(see below)* is a good start. As you seek out any particular objects in the 100 or so galleries, you will be diverted by enough intriguing displays to justify future visits.

The British Museum (tel: 7323 8000; www.thebritishmuseum.ac.uk; Thurs–Fri 10am–8.30pm; free admission) is the most traditional of institutions, with most objects in glass cases and few buttons and levers for children to manipulate, but it is rarely boring. The best time to visit is soon after opening, before the crowds arrive.

Below:1991 bronze by Igor Mitoraj, at the main entrance Bottom: 18th-century collector Charles Townley and friends

HISTORY

The idea of transferring the private collections of rich men to public ownership in order to guarantee

their continuity – and, with luck, perpetuate the donor's name – originated in 16th-century Italy, and it was central to the birth of the British Museum in 1759. Then, as now, British politicians were loath to spend public money on financing cultural awareness and had to be pressured by enterprising individuals. In the end, the funds to build and stock the museum were raised through a lottery. The collection was initially based in Montagu House, a handsome 17th-century mansion, since demolished, slightly south of today's museum in Bloomsbury. Today's imposing and dignified neoclassical museum, designed by Sir Robert Smirke, was begun in 1826, with new wings being added piecemeal over the next quarter of a century.

THE GREAT COURT

In 1857, the celebrated Reading Room – where Karl Marx researched *Das Kapital* – was added in the central courtyard to house most of the museum's immense library. In 1997, the British Library was relocated to new premises on the Euston Road, allowing the British Museum to make radical changes to its overcrowded building. The most radical change was the glassing over of the Great Court, the area around the Reading Room in the centre of the building. The curators see the Great Court not just as an essential improvement to the museum's existing facilities but as a free public space in its own right. Even as a superior place to shelter from the rain, it's hard to beat.

Shops, cafés and a new restaurant have been added, together with a few striking artefacts such as the majestic Lion of Cnidos and an Easter Island statue. It is a spectacular experience.

THE READING ROOM

Readers here included Marx, Lenin, George Bernard Shaw, Thomas Hardy, Rudyard Kipling and Oscar Wilde. To gain access to its majestic interior, they needed readers' tickets, but today, following the relocation of the British Library, it is open to all. The main attraction is the room

Star Attraction
● **The Great Court**

Architectural wonder
The hi-tech panelling of the Great Court's roof contains 3,312 unique glass triangles. It blends with the classicism of the 19th-century buildings to create the largest covered public space in Europe.

Below: the Great Court
Bottom: the Reading Room

Plan
on page
64

*The gilded inner coffin of the
priestess Henutmehyt, from
around 1290 BC*

itself, described by the *Publishers' Circular*
when it opened in 1857 as 'a circular temple of
marvellous dimensions, rich in blue, and white,
and gold.'

THE HIGHLIGHTS

Although the British Museum's collections span
2 million years, it is best known for its antiquities
from Greece and Egypt and these dominate the
highlights which should be seen on any first visit.

The Egyptian mummies

Rooms 62–63, on the upper floors, are the rooms
to see first, simply because they can get wildly
overcrowded as the day goes on. They're worth
seeing, too: thanks to the enthusiastic plundering
of 19th-century explorers, this is the richest
collection of Egyptian funerary art outside
Egypt. A glass case in Room 64 contains the
body of a truly ancient Egyptian, his flesh
preserved in the sands for 5,400 years. He is
familiarly known as Ginger.

The Sculptures of the Parthenon

Commonly known as the Elgin Marbles, these
have their own spacious quarters on the main floor
(Room 18). Carved in the 5th century BC for the
Temple of Athena Parthenos, patron goddess of
Athens, these are, even in their damaged state,
some of the greatest sculptures ever created, their
muscular detail and fluidity of movement airily
transcending their origins as blocks of marble.

The Rosetta Stone

From the west side of the Great Court, enter
Room 4 and turn left to find the granite tablet
from the 2nd century BC which provided the key
in the 19th century to deciphering ancient
Egypt's hieroglyphic script.

The Nereid Monument

Room 17 contains the imposing facade of this
4th-century monument from Xanthos in Turkey,
destroyed by an earthquake and reconstructed by
the British Museum.

The Mausoleum of Halikarnassos

This giant tomb (Room 21), finished around 351
BC in southwest Turkey, was one of the seven
wonders of the ancient world.

The Sutton Hoo Ship Burial

Room 42, on the first floor, contains the richest treasure ever dug from British soil, an early 7th-century longboat likely to have been the burial chamber of Raedwald, an East Anglian king. A rich hoard of weapons, armour, coins, bowls and jewellery has survived.

The Lewis Chessmen

Also in Room 42 are these 82 elaborately carved 12th-century chess pieces, probably made in Norway and found on the Isle of Lewis in Scotland's Outer Hebrides.

Lindow Man

Room 50 is the final resting place of one of Britain's most senior citizens, found in a peat bog, Lindow Moss, in Cheshire in 1984. The 2,000-year-old body, dubbed Pete Marsh, was identifed as the victim of a Druidic sacrifice.

The Benin bronzes

In Room 25, in the basement, are around five dozen of the 900 brass plaques found in Benin City, Nigeria, in 1897. Probably cast in the 16th century to clad the wooden pillars of the palace, they depict court life and ritual in great detail.

The Cassiobury Park Turret Clock

The intricate workings of this 1610 weight-driven clock, originally installed in a country

> **Tours worth taking**
> Ninety-minute tours of the museum's highlights take place daily at 10.30am, 1.30pm, 2.30pm and 3.30pm. Briefer one-hour Focus tours are also held, and audio sets can be hired to provide a self-guided tour of 50 key objects.

Below: Lindow Man
Bottom: a frieze from the Sculptures of the Parthenon

Plan below

house in Hertfordshire, are fascinating to behold. The museum's remarkable collection of clocks and watches is in Room 44.

THE MAIN COLLECTIONS

Greece and Rome

The museum's vast holdings from the Classical world are divided between Rooms 11–23 on the ground floor (the larger exhibits) and Rooms 69–73 on the first floor. Room 70 contains the Portland Vase, a superbly crafted cameo-glass vessel from the early 1st century.

Ancient Egypt

There are two main collections: sculptures, on the ground floor; and mummies on the first floor. The ancient Egyptians stocked tombs with everything the departed might need for the next (strikingly similar) life, and the country's dry climate preserved many of these objects.

Ancient Near East

Among the highlights are a number of clay tablets with cuneiform inscriptions, one of the

Below: ivory mask from Benin, Nigeria

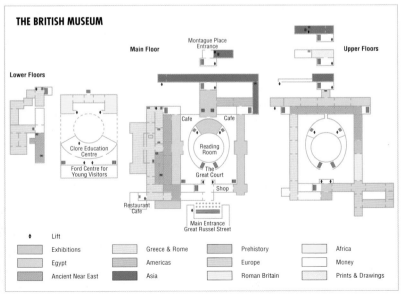

THE BRITISH MUSEUM

Main Floor

Montague Place Entrance

Upper Floors

Lower Floors

Cafe   Cafe

Clore Education Centre

Reading Room

Ford Centre for Young Visitors

The Great Court

Shop

Restaurant Cafe

Main Entrance Great Russel Street

✦ Lift		
Exhibitions	Greece & Rome	Prehistory	Africa
Egypt	Americas	Europe	Money
Ancient Near East	Asia	Roman Britain	Prints & Drawings

oldest forms of writing. One, nearly 5,000 years old, records the delivery of barley to a temple. Among somewhat later objects, the highlight is probably the series of carved Assyrian reliefs.

Early Europe

The elaborate, highly crafted Celtic artefacts are remarkable. Shields, coins, a wide variety of jewellery and drinking vessels testify to the vigour and achievements of Celtic culture. Room 49 has a wide range of Roman treasures.

Medieval and Modern Europe

Apart from the Sutton Hoo treasure *(see page 63)*, medieval objects include a series of richly decorated ecclesiastical artefacts. A highlight is an intricately patterned and decorated 12th-century gilt cross from Germany.

Africa

The Sainsbury African Galleries in the basement combine ancient and modern, showing how cultural traditions are still alive today. This is one of the most colourful collections in the museum.

Asia

The museum's collections of Chinese, Japanese and Korean artefacts are astonishingly large and varied, with a series of vast galleries given over to them (33–34 on the ground floor; 67 and 91–94 on the first floor). Exhibits from India include some exquisite bronzes.

The Americas

The museum has superb collections from Central and North America in Rooms 26–27 on the ground floor. There are a number of hugely impressive Olmec statues and other works from around 1000 BC, as well as magnificent carved Mayan slabs from the 8th century AD.

Money and Medals

A collection of 750,000 coins dates from the 7th century BC to the present day, and there are notes dating back to 14th-century China (Room 68).

Prints and Drawings

For conservation and space reasons, only a fraction of the museum's 3 million works on paper are displayed at any one time. Highlights include Old Master prints and drawings, and satires of the 18th and 19th centuries.

Top: the Portland Vase
Above: helmet from the Sutton Hoo Ship Burial
Below: a stoneware figure from the Ming Dynasty

Map below

11: The City

Museum of London – Barbican – Mansion House – Bank of England – Monument

Below: the City's coat of arms

CITY OF LONDON

For most of the capital's 2,000-year history, the 'Square Mile' between St Paul's Cathedral and the Tower *was* London. Still known as 'The City', it has its own local government, led by a Lord Mayor, and its own police force. The network of medieval alleys and back streets is still evident, but today's tall buildings hum with banks of computers processing a large chunk of international finance. Teeming with life on weekdays, the City is virtually deserted at weekends.

Lord Mayor's Show
On the second Saturday in November, the Lord Mayor in a gilded coach leads a ceremonial procession, complete with floats and military bands, from the Guildhall to the Law Courts in Strand.

MUSEUM OF LONDON

To absorb the area's history, walk north up Aldersgate Street to the ★★ **Museum of London** ❼❸ (Mon–Sat 10am–5.50pm, Sun noon–5.50pm; free). It holds more than a million objects in its stores, making it the world's largest urban history museum. Aside from important prehistoric and

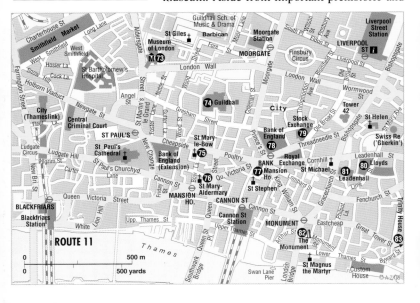

Roman collections, it has a vast archaeological archive, a costume and decorative arts collection, and a photographic archive of 280,000 images. Most of the museum's collections, including all post-1914 exhibits, are in storage.

London's history is traced chronologically across two floors, from prehistory to the Tudors and Stuarts at the entrance level and from the late Stuarts to the early 20th century at the lower level. The same thematic threads run through each period – architecture, trade and industry, transport, health, multiculturalism, religion, fashions, leisure pursuits. There are lots of detailed information panels; you may find that, an hour into your visit, you're still with the Romans. Here are some highlights from each section:

Roman London. This gallery has a hoard of gold coins (1st–2nd century AD) found buried in a safety deposit box near Fenchurch Street and the gilded arms of what must have been a life-size statue of a god or emperor.

Tudors to the early Stuarts. The civil war collection includes Oliver Cromwell's death mask and bible, but more captivating is the cabinet filled with the glittering Cheapside Hoard. In 1912, a workman digging in Cheapside hit on a box containing 230 pieces of finely crafted jewellery set with precious stones. The treasure is thought to have belonged to a goldsmith forced to hide his precious stock during the civil war.

Restoration London. Changes in society are examined with exhibits on music and theatre, taverns and early tourism, fashion and the calico craze, interior decor and tableware. The star attraction on the lower level is the Lord Mayor's gilded coach (1757), an elaborate if gaudy display of the exquisite craftsmanship that characterised the age. It is taken out of the museum every November for the Lord Mayor's Show.

World City Gallery. This runs from the French Revolution to World War I. Exhibits include the Duke of Wellington's boots, hat and duelling pistols, a jewelled sword presented to Admiral Lord Nelson, Queen Victoria's parliamentary robes and one of the first motorised taxis.

Star attraction
● **Museum of London**

Below: Roman mosaic found during construction work
Bottom: detail of 'London from Southwark', painted around 1630 by an unknown artist

Map on page 66

Roman London
Little remains of the 20ft high (6-metre) Roman Wall which enclosed the City 2,000 years ago, but fragments can be seen at London Wall, Noble Street, Cooper's Row and in the Museum of London.

Below: gold bars at the Bank of England Museum
Bottom: the Guildhall

THE GUILDHALL

Adjacent to the museum is the **Barbican** complex, which combines apartments, schools, shops and an arts centre staging concerts and plays. To the south, on Gresham Street, the ★ **Guildhall** ❼❹ (9.30am–5pm, closed Sun in winter), centre of the City's government, has a magnificent Great Hall and impressive displays of banners and coats of arms. Parts of the building date to the 15th century, but much has been restored. The adjacent **Guildhall Art Gallery** (Mon–Sat 10am–5pm, Sun noon–4pm; fee) displays selections of the Corporation's 4,000 paintings, many dealing with London. The **Guildhall Clock Museum** (Mon–Fri 9.30am–4.30pm; free) is a room filled with intricate timepieces from the 17th century on.

Medieval London was packed with churches, and many survive. On Cheapside, **St Mary-le-Bow** ❼❺, a Norman church restored by Sir Christopher Wren in 1670–83, is noted for its Bow Bells, within the sound of which you must be born to qualify as a true cockney. Some Roman bricks have been incorporated in the crypt. Wren also rebuilt **St Mary Aldermary** ❼❻ on Queen Victoria Street in a neo-Gothic style.

Cheapside and Queen Victoria Street converge at Bank, the City's major crossroads, flanked by significant buildings. The Renaissance-style **Mansion House** ❼❼, the Lord Mayor's official

residence, has magnificent rooms but these are not open to the public. Behind it is the church of **St Stephen Walbrook** (1096), with a dome reminiscent of St Paul's and an altar by Henry Moore.

Bank takes its name from the ★ ★ **Bank of England** ㉘, originally erected between 1788 and 1833 by Sir John Soane but largely rebuilt between 1925 and 1939. The **Bank of England Museum** (Mon–Fri 10am–5pm; free) has a splendid setting and brings finance to life surprisingly well with displays and interactive terminals.

The **Royal Exchange**, which houses the London International Financial Futures Exchange, and the **London Stock Exchange** ㉚, along Threadneedle Street, are not open to visitors. Nor is the **Lloyd's of London** ㉚ insurance building in Lime Street, but its modernistic 1986 design by Richard Rogers is well worth a look. Close by is **Leadenhall** ㉛, once a wholesale market for poultry and game and now a striking complex of restaurants and shops.

Connoisseurs of old churches should check out **St Mary Woolnoth**, a 13th-century church in Lombard Street rebuilt by Nicholas Hawksmoor in 1716–27, **St Andrew Undershaft**, a much rebuilt 12th-century church in Leadenhall Street, and **St Katharine Cree**, a 13th-century church in the same street which survived the 1666 Great Fire and where the painter Hans Holbein, a plague victim, was buried in 1543.

THE MONUMENT

You can view many of Christopher Wren's 56 spires by climbing the 311 steps to the top of the 200-ft (67-metre) ★ **Monument** ㉜ in Monument Yard (Apr–Sept Mon–Fri 9am–5.40pm, Sat & Sun 2–5.40pm; Oct–Mar Mon–Sat 9am–4pm). The Roman Doric column was designed by Wren to commemorate the nine victims of the Great Fire, which destoyed 13,200 houses and 89 churches.

Head along to Lower Thames Street to Tower Hill and the **Tower of London** *(see overleaf)*. At Trinity Square is the elegant **Trinity House** ㉝ (1793), which controls all lighthouses, buoys and beacons off the coasts of England and Wales.

Star attraction
● **The Bank of England**

Below: Leadenhall Market
Bottom: Lloyd's of London

Plan below

Detail from Thomas and William Daniell's 1805 painting of the Tower

12: The Tower of London

The bulk of the ★★★ **Tower of London** ❸❹ (tel: 7709 0765. www.hrp.org.uk; Mar–Oct Mon–Sat 9am–5pm, Sun 10am–5pm; Nov–Feb Tues–Sat 9am–4pm, Sun–Mon 10am–4pm; fee) is a stolid reminder of how power was once exercised. Two of Henry VIII's wives, Anne Boleyn and Catherine Howard, were beheaded here in 1536 and 1542. So were Sir Thomas More, Henry's principled Lord Chancellor (1535), and Sir Walter Raleigh, the last of the great Elizabethan adventurers (1618). The uncrowned Edward V, aged 12, and his 10-year-old brother Richard were murdered here in 1483, allegedly on the orders of Richard III. William Penn, the future founder of Pennsylvania, was imprisoned here in 1669, and the diarist Samuel Pepys in 1679. In 1941, Rudolph Hess, Germany's Deputy Führer, was locked in the Tower.

Encircled by a moat (now dry), with 22 towers, the Tower of London, begun by William the Conqueror in 1078, is Britain's most celebrated military monument. Yet, given that so much of

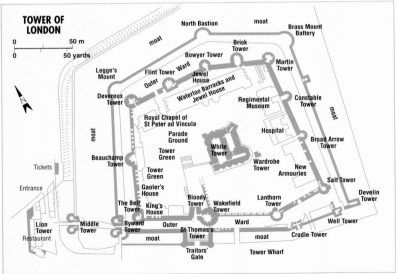

TOWER OF LONDON

0 ___ 50 m
0 ___ 50 yards

N

moat

North Bastion
moat
Brass Mount Battery
Brick Tower
Bowyer Tower
Martin Tower
Legge's Mount
Flint Tower
Ward
Outer
Jewel House
Waterloo Barracks and Jewel House
Regimental Museum
Constable Tower
Devereux Tower
Royal Chapel of St Peter ad Vincula
Parade Ground
Hospital
Broad Arrow Tower
moat
White Tower
Beauchamp Tower
Tower Green
Wardrobe Tower
New Armouries
Salt Tower
Tickets
Tower Green
Gaoler's House
Bloody Tower
Lanthorn Tower
Develin Tower
Entrance
The Bell Tower
King's House
Wakefield Tower
Well Tower
Lion Tower
Middle Tower
Byward Tower
Outer
Ward
Cradle Tower
Restaurant
moat
St Thomas's Tower
moat
Traitors' Gate
Tower Wharf

the country's turbulent history was played out within these walls, it conspicuously lacks the romantic aura that many visitors expect. The reason is that, until comparatively recently, its buildings were functional – as well as serving as a fort, arsenal, palace and prison, it also contained at various times a treasury, public record office, observatory, royal mint and zoo. As a result, it was frequently remodelled and renovated, especially in the 19th century, so that many floors and staircases, for example, look more modern than medieval. But then, how could the boards that Henry VIII trod hope to survive the footfalls of 2½ million tourists a year?

Any sense of awe is also undermined by the brightly uniformed 'Beefeaters', the 40 yeoman warders who live with their families in houses within the grounds and act as tour guides (their nickname may derive from the French *buffetier*, a servant). Although all have served in the armed forces for at least 22 years, some have ardently embraced showbiz, apparently auditioning for the role of pantomime villain by alternating jocular banter with visitors and melodramatically delivered descriptions of torture and beheadings.

Given that the Tower's 18 acres (7.3 hectares) contain enough important buildings and collections to occupy three hours, you may prefer to skip the one-hour Beefeater-led tour and strike out on your own, relying on your imagination and the comprehensive official guidebook or free map. An audio guide can also be hired.

THE SIGHTS TO SEE

Traitor's Gate

After entering through Middle Tower, you pass through Byward Tower; both date from the 13th century but have been much rebuilt. Mint Street, in whose 18th-century houses some of the Beefeaters live, is on the left. Ahead, past the Bell Tower (1190s) is Water Lane. Along this lane, on the right, is Traitor's Gate, the water entrance created by Edward I in 1275–79; barges would carry suspected traitors down the Thames and through this gate.

Star attraction
● **Tower of London**

Below: the Beefeaters
Bottom: Traitor's Gate

Plan
on page
70

*Below: the Imperial
State Crown
Bottom: Tudor encounter for
the tourists on Tower Green*

The Medieval Palace

This is the residential part of the Tower, used by monarchs when they lived here. Parts of the Wakefield Tower (1220–40) have been furnished in 13th-century style, complete with a throne copied from the Coronation Chair in Westminster Abbey.

The Crown Jewels

These are displayed in the neo-Gothic Waterloo Barracks. At the centre of the display are a dozen crowns and a glittering array of swords, sceptres and orbs used on royal occasions. The Imperial State Crown, made in 1937, has 2,868 diamonds and is topped with an 11th-century sapphire. A moving walkway speeds you past the treasures.

The White Tower

The oldest part of the fortress, the White Tower was probably designed in 1078 and has walls 15ft (5 metres) thick. Virtually every part has been refurbished or rebuilt over the centuries. There are extensive displays from the Royal Armouries: shields, suits of armour, cutlasses, broadswords, pistols, matchlock muskets, mortars and cannon. The Line of Kings, first recorded at the Tower in 1660, is a row of 10 full-size sculpted horses with royal armour from the 11th to the 17th centuries.

Tower Green

This grassy area gives access (but only as part of tours) to the much rebuilt Chapel Royal of St Peter ad Vincula which contains memorials and ornate monuments. In front of the chapel is the Scaffold Site where nobles were beheaded. Close by, the Beauchamp Tower (1281) housed high-ranking prisoners, some for many years.

The Bloody Tower

Built in the 1220s, this housed the most eminent prisoners, including Archbishop Thomas Cranmer (in 1553–54) and Sir Walter Raleigh (1603–16). The rooms are now furnished as they might have been during Raleigh's internment.

The Royal Fusiliers Museum

Displays of medals, paintings and uniforms follow the regiment's campaigns from its founding in 1685 to its recent peacekeeping involvement in the Balkans and Northern Ireland.

13: Southwark

★★Tower Bridge ㉟, a triumph of Victorian engineering opened in 1894, is still raised regularly to allow ships into the Pool of London. The **Tower Bridge Experience** (Apr–Oct 10am–6.30pm, Nov–Mar 9.30am–6pm; entrance near the northern bank; fee) recounts the crossing's history through audiovisual and interactive displays. Raised walkways give a spectacular view.

The oval-shaped glass building on the south bank of the river, facing the Tower, is the headquarters of the **Greater London Authority**, and the Norman Foster design has been variously described as a clenched fist and a glass testicle. The GLA is the body responsible for much of the city's administration. The mayor is based here.

The old warehouses east of Tower Bridge contain a gourmet's delight. The gourmet in question is Habitat founder Sir Terence Conran, who has opened up five restaurants in the biscuit-coloured **Butler's Wharf**. The **Design Museum ㊱** (Mon–Fri 11.30am–6pm, Sat–Sun 10.30am–6pm; fee), also inspired by Conran, has an exhibition of influential design and artefacts, mainly 20th-century, as well as hands-on displays.

Westward along the river is **★★HMS *Belfast* ㊲**, a gun-bristling cruiser, and last of the warships to have seen action in World War II (daily

Map below

Star attractions
● Tower Bridge
● HMS Belfast

Tower Bridge

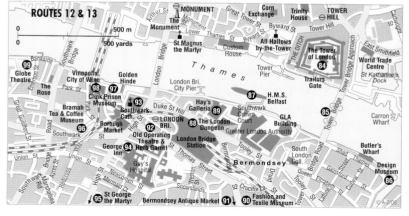

Map
on page
73

*Below: the London Dungeon
Centre: Britain at War Museum
Bottom: HMS Belfast*

10am–6pm, Oct–Apr 10am–5pm; fee). Its tour ranges from the bridge to the engine rooms. The present three-span **London Bridge**, dating from 1967–72, is the latest of many on this site. The first bridge, probably made of wood, was built by the Romans around AD50. In Tooley Street, which runs beside London Bridge Station, the **London Dungeon** ⓼ includes ghoulish exhibits of the Black Death, the Great Fire of 1666 and Jack the Ripper's exploits. A few doors away, **Winston Churchill's Britain at War Museum** recreates the sounds and smells of the blitz through special effects. School parties have great fun trying on helmets and gas masks and there's a lot of 1940s memorabilia. Opposite is **Hay's Galleria** ⓽, a small leisure mall carved out of a former tea wharf.

A few minutes' walk away, at 83 Bermondsey Street, Zandra Rhodes, 'high priestess of pink', is creating the **Fashion and Textile Museum** ⓴ (7403 0222), emphasising the work of British designers from the 1950s onwards.

Further along the street is **Bermondsey Antiques Market** ⓺, best visited early on Friday.

Closer to London Bridge, at 9A St Thomas Street, the **Old Operating Theatre & Herb Garret** ⓽ (daily 10.30am–5pm, tel: 8806 4325) is the only surviving 19th-century operating theatre in Britain. It offers a gruesome but fascinating insight into both the social history of

Southwark and the sometimes fearsome medical techniques of the day. The Herb Garret displays herbs and equipment used in the preparation of 19th-century medicines.

★★**Southwark Cathedral ㉓**, hemmed in by the railway, has a lovely interior and is one of London's great historic churches. In the 12th century it was a priory church, and it has a Norman north door, early Gothic work and a number of medieval ornaments. A memorial to Shakespeare in the south aisle, paid for by public subscription in 1912, shows the bard reclining in front of a frieze of 16th-century Bankside. Above it is a modern (1954) stained-glass window depicting characters from his plays. Shakespeare was a parishioner for several years. John Harvard, who gave his name to the American university, was baptised here, and is commemorated in the Harvard Chapel. There's a modern memorial to Sam Wanamaker, the American actor who championed the rebuilding of Shakespeare's Globe Theatre *(see next page)*.

Borough Market, outside the cathedral, is a wholesale fruit and vegetable market dating from the 13th century. Trade begins in earnest at around 2am. On Fridays and Saturdays it turns into an organic and gourmet retail market. A two-minute diversion down Southwark Street, past the splendidly Victorian **Hop Exchange** (now offices) is the small and charming **Bramah Tea and Coffee Museum ㉖**, which gives a history of the long-established trade in London (10am–6pm).

DICKENS TERRITORY

On Borough High Street, at number 77, is the 17th-century ★**George Inn ㉔**, the only remaining galleried coaching inn in London. It was mentioned by Dickens in *Little Dorrit* and is now owned by the National Trust. Further down Borough High Street, the ★**Church of St George the Martyr ㉕** is sometimes known as 'Little Dorrit's Church' because Dickens's heroine was baptised and married there. There are recitals at 1pm on Thursdays (free but donations welcome), when you are invited to bring a packed lunch.

Star attraction
● **Southwark Cathedral**

Below: Southwark Cathedral
Bottom: the George Inn

Map on page 73

Below: Winchester Palace
Bottom: the Italy display
in Vinopolis

From Borough Market, cut down Stoney Street to reach **St Mary Overie Dock**, which contains a full-size replica of Sir Francis Drake's galleon, the *Golden Hinde* (daily 9am–sunset; fee). The Devon-built ship, launched in 1973, is the only replica to have completed a circumnavigation of the globe. It has thus clocked up more nautical miles than the original, in which Drake set sail in 1577 on the greatest piratical voyage in English history. Down Clink Street, the **Clink Prison Museum ⑰** recalls the area's prostitution and displays working armoury (10am–6pm daily). Beside each exhibit, plaques give information on aspects of prison life and history. The prison was founded by the powerful Bishops of Winchester, who made their own laws and regulated local brothels. A single gable wall remains of **Winchester Palace**, their former London residence.

At the end of Clink Street **Vinopolis, City of Wine ⑱** occupies 2½ acres (1 hectare) of cathedral-like spaces under railway arches. This sprawling attraction offers a visual wine tour through exhibits of the world's major wine regions. Individual audio units and earphones give access to four hours of recorded commentary in six languages, and the admission fee to the tour includes five wine tastings. Opposite it is the **Anchor Inn**, a maze of passageways combining a minstrels' gallery, oak beams and dark staircases. Dr Samuel Johnson, of dictionary fame, drank here.

BANKSIDE'S PLAYERS

This historic area, Bankside, grew up in competition with the City opposite, but by the 16th century had become a den of vice, famous for brothels, bear and bull-baiting pits, prize fights and the first playhouses, including ★★**Shakespeare's Globe ⑲**. The replica of the 1599 building opened in 1996 and is worth a visit even if you're not seeing a play (guided tours every half-hour 9.15am–12.15pm; fee). The Globe has been painstakingly re-created using the original methods of construction – though, bearing in mind that the original Globe burned down when a stage cannon set the thatch alight, today's thatched roof is fire-resistant. The season of the open-air galleried theatre runs from May to September (box office tel: 7401 9919). The theatre can absorb 1,500 people – 600 standing (and liable to get wet if it rains) and the rest seated. The wooden benches can feel distinctly hard by Act III, but you can rent cushions.

The fascinating **Shakespeare's Globe Exhibition**, to the right of the theatre, is well worth a visit. There are traditional displays, but touch screens and hands-on exhibits provide the fun element. You can, for example, rehearse one of a number of Shakespearian scenes, reading your character's lines from a screen in response to a recording of actors declaiming the other parts; the whole scene is then played back and your performance is accorded a gratifying round of recorded applause.

Shakespeare also acted at the **Rose Theatre**, whose foundations were discovered close by in 1989. Turn down New Globe Walk (by the Globe's box office) and then left into Park Street. At Number 56, the **Rose Exhibition** (daily 10am–5pm; fee), a sound-and-light presentation narrated by Sir Ian McKellan, tells the story of the Rose, Bankside's first theatre, built in 1587.

From here you can cross the river to St Paul's Cathedral by the Millennium Bridge or continue towards the South Bank *(see pages 22–26).*

Star attraction
● **Shakespeare's Globe**

> **The Financial Times**
> The large letters FT displayed on the black glass of Number One, Southwark Bridge, identify it as the HQ of the *Financial Times*. The paper first appeared on 13 February 1888 and turned pink five years later. In 1989, with the advent of new printing technology, the FT moved from its previous home near St Paul's Cathedral to this practical six-storey block. The paper isn't actually printed here – that happens in a Docklands plant and in 14 other cities around the world.

Shakespeare's Globe

Map below

14: Waterloo and the Imperial War Museum

Turning down Waterloo Road from the marble bulk of Waterloo Station brings you to the elegant ★**Old Vic**, which since 1818 has been a music hall, the first home of the National Theatre and now a repertory theatre. Further down The Cut, the **Young Vic** is an open space auditorium which stages more experimental work.

Waterloo Station

Turn right at the Old Vic junction into Baylis Road and bear right into **Lower Marsh**, This contains the remnant of what was in the 19th century London's longest street market. At the end of the street, turn left into Westminster Bridge Road and then into Lambeth Road.

★★★ IMPERIAL WAR MUSEUM ⓾

This stately building on Lambeth Road (tel: 7416 5439; www.iwm.org.uk; 10am–6pm; free) opened in 1815 to house the Bethlem Royal Hospital for the insane, popularly known as Bedlam and an inspired choice for a museum chronicling the horrors of modern warfare.

The museum has expanded its remit from the purely military to include a rolling programme

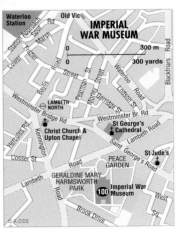

of exhibitions, many aimed at young people. These cover many aspects of modern history, often only loosely connected with conflict – from code breaking and refugees to fashion and sport.

The main hall contains the expected guns, tanks and fighter planes. Exhibitions on the two world wars, which include artefacts, art, photography, and film and sound recordings, weave an atmosphere as close as possible to the mood of the time, while interactive screens give access to further information. Looking at a letter informing a father of his son's death brings it all down to the human level. Official material includes Field-Marshal Bernard Montgomery's papers, Hitler's will and the overoptimistic 'piece of paper' that prime minister Neville Chamberlain waved on his return from meeting Adolf Hitler in Munich in 1938.

The Blitz and Trench 'experiences' may appeal more to children than adults. The Trench is inexplicably dark and not especially realistic, though the sense of smell is quite effective: an unpleasant musty odour gives way to the sharpness of disinfectant as you pass the hospital tent. You may have to queue for the Blitz Experience, which works better. The darkness in which you wait for air raids is atmospheric and recorded announcements help to create tension.

On the first floor is an aeroplane fuselage that you can walk through, plus a Secret War exhibit on counter-intelligence. The second floor holds a major collection of 20th-century war art.

Occupying the next two floors is the **Holocaust Exhibition**, which will take you a good hour to look around and sample the large amount of video and film available. Be warned: this is a harrowing exhibition, with a lower age limit of 13. It is built around the testimonies of a selection of survivors. Film footage accompanies the stories, as does rare and important historical material. Larger items include a section of a deportation railcar, the entrance to a gas chamber, a dissection table, shoes collected from victims of the gas chambers, and a large model of part of Auschwitz.

Star attraction
● **Imperial War Museum**

*Below: Imperial War Museum
Bottom: the museum's
Large Exhibits Hall*

Map below

15: South London

Blackheath – Brixton – Dulwich – Greenwich

BLACKHEATH

One of London's neat middle-class 'villages', this is a mix of small shops, restaurants and expensive houses. The windy heath is where Henry V was welcomed home after beating the French at Agincourt in 1415, and it was here that James I introduced the Scottish game of golf to England in 1608. Overlooking the heath is the Paragon, a crescent of restored colonnaded houses. **St Michael's Church** (1829) has a severely tapering spire known as 'the needle of Kent'.

BRIXTON

It is not the architecture but the people who give Brixton its character, colour and energy. The population is around 60 percent white, and the balance includes a high proportion of Cypriots, Vietnamese, Chinese, African and Caribbean

North and South

North Londoners have tended to feel superior to those south of the Thames. In Tudor times, they consigned brothels and theatres (then considered disreputable) to the south bank and built jails there. Polluting industries, such as tanning and brewing, were based there. London's Industrial Revolution was powered by workers housed in a maze of neighbourhoods south of the river that still confuses many North Londoners.

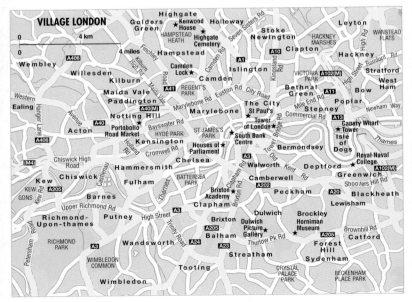

people. Its laid-back attitude to recreational drugs gets Brixton a bad press, but it attracts young professionals keen to own their own homes.

Plotting the presence of black people in Britain are the **Black Cultural Archives** (378 Coldharbour Lane, tel: 7738 4591; Mon–Fri by appointment only; free), a large collection of artefacts and memorabilia used primarily by researchers.

Brixton Market (Mon–Sat 8am–6pm, except Wed when it ends at 3pm), running from Electric Avenue to Brixton Station Road, mixes Caribbean produce with traditional fruit, vegetables and fish, plus stalls of secondhand clothes, music and general junk. There's a real community buzz here, but keep any valuables out of sight.

Nightlife is lively here. The five-screen **Ritzy** cinema in Coldharbour Lane is popular, as are dance clubs such as the **Fridge** (1 Town Hall Parade) and bar-clubs such as **Bug Bar** (Brixton Hill) and **Dogstar** (389 Coldharbour Lane).

DULWICH

With leafy streets, elegant houses and a spacious park, Dulwich is an oasis of rural calm. It is largely the creation of one man, Edward Alleyn, an actor-manager who bought land in the area in 1605 and established an estate to administer a chapel, almshouses and a school for the poor.

Today, the estate has more than 15,000 homes, Dulwich College, Alleyn's School and James Allen's Girls' School. The last village farm disappeared only in 1954.

Dulwich College, which schooled the writers P. G. Wodehouse and Raymond Chandler, spawned the ★★ **Dulwich Picture Gallery** (Gallery Road, tel: 8693 5254, Tues–Fri 10am–5pm, Sat–Sun 11am–5pm, free on Fri) by combining Alleyn's original collection with a bequest of valuable paintings originally intended for a Polish National Gallery but diverted when the King of Poland was forced to abdicate. The magnificent building was designed by Sir John Soane and opened in 1814 as the country's first major public art gallery. It contains important works by Rembrandt,

Star attraction
● **Dulwich Picture Gallery**

Below: Brixton Market
Bottom: Raphael's St Francis of Assisi at Dulwich Picture Gallery

Map on page 80

Rubens, Van Dyck, Gainsborough and Murillo (*see page 97*).

A mile to the east, the ★★ **Horniman Museum** (100 London Road, Forest Hill, tel: 8699 1872 Mon–Sat 10.30am–5.30pm, Sun 2–5.30pm) is one of south London's unsung treasures. Combining rich collections of ethnography and natural history, it was founded in 1901 by a wealthy tea merchant, Frederick Horniman and is set in 16 acres (6.5 hectares) of landscaped parkland, with great views across London. Highlights include a spectacular collection of African masks, exquisite bronze plaques from Benin in west Africa, stuffed mammals and birds, an aquarium with an emphasis on conservation, and a reptiles area. You can play some of the unusual and historical musical instruments from a vast collection.

Below: Horniman Museum
Bottom: Greenwich Market

GREENWICH

A good way of getting to Greenwich is the time-honoured tradition of arriving at this maritime centre by water. Boats leave Westminster Pier daily from 10am (10.40am in winter) and take about 50 minutes. The best alternative is via the Docklands Light Railway.

By the river is the vast **Millennium Dome**, built to house a one-year exhibition for the millennium; this was a financial and critical

failure and a permanent use for the dome is still to be decided. A more lasting success has been Sir Christopher Wren's ★★★ **Old Royal Observatory** (10am–5pm; free), where Greenwich Mean Time was established in 1884. It has Britain's largest refracting telescope and a fine display of time-keeping ephemera, including John Harrison's famous clocks whose story was told in Dava Sobel's 1995 book *Longitude*. A brass rule on the ground marks the line between the Eastern and Western hemispheres, making it possible to have a foot in both worlds. It's a steep climb to the observatory, but the views are great.

In dry dock on the waterfront is the *Cutty Sark* (10am–6pm, Sun noon–6pm; 5pm in winter; fee), a sailing ship from the great days of the speedy 19th-century tea clippers. Below decks is a re-constructed cargo, a collection of figureheads and a compelling video of archive film.

The ★★★ **National Maritime Museum** (daily 10am–5pm; free) displays an unrivalled coll-ection of maritime art and artefacts in 16 galleries built around a spectacular courtyard. The ground-floor galleries cover great explorers, the mass migrations from Europe to America, cargo ship-ping, London's naval heritage, and naval clothing.

On the first floor, exhibits cover the expansion of the British Empire, marine art and the history of the Navy. A giant sphere in the courtyard area projects images of the sea onto 32 screens, showing both the beauty of the oceans and our destruction of them.

On the third floor, a whole gallery is dedicated to Admiral Horatio Nelson (1758–1805). The museum's most prized possession is the uniform coat he was wearing when he was killed in the Battle of Trafalgar on board the *Victory*. The bullet hole at the shoulder and the bloodstains on his stockings are clearly visible. This is the floor that will amuse restless children. A large area is given over to two interactive galleries: the All Hands gallery, where you can send a morse code message, have a go at gunnery target practice or try out a diver's suit; and the Bridge, where you can take the helm of a Viking longship or try to steer a virtual paddle steamer.

The ★ **Queen's House**, now used to showcase

Star attractions
● Horniman Museum
● Old Royal Observatory
● National Maritime Museum

Below: where time begins
Bottom: the Cutty Sark

Map on page 80

Below: historical re-enactment at Greenwich
Bottom: the Queen's House

the museum's art collections, was completed in 1637. With its high windows and Ionic columns, it was England's first classical Renaissance building.

The elegant ★ **Royal Naval College**, begun by Wren in 1696, was built in two halves to preserve the view from Queen's House to the river. The Painted Hall and the chapel can be visited.

The heart of Greenwich lies just to the west of the park, where a covered market and neighbouring Greenwich Church Street are especially lively on a Sunday. In one of Greenwich's elegant period houses is the **Fan Museum** (12 Croom's Hill, tel: 8305 1441, Tues–Sat 11am–5pm, Sun noon–5pm; fee) with an unusual collection of hand-held fans from fashion and the stage.

You can catch a riverboat downstream to see the ★ **Thames Barrier**, whose massive gates swing shut if there's a danger of London flooding.

Beyond is **Woolwich,** once the Royal Navy's dockyards and arsenal. The main attraction today at the Royal Arsenal is ★★**Firepower** (tel: 8855 7755; daily 10am–5pm; frequent overground trains from Waterloo East, Charing Cross, London Bridge and Cannon Street). The centrepiece of this military museum is the ground-shaking "Field of Fire", which puts viewers in the midst of battle. There is also a large two-level gunnery gallery and 'have a go' simulators show visitors what it's like being a gunner in the field of war.

16: West & Southwest London

Notting Hill – Wimbledon – Richmond – Kew

NOTTING HILL

Every Saturday morning tidal waves of tourists emerge from Notting Hill Gate Tube station and make the seven-minute trek to ★★**Portobello Road**. Built on the site of a pig farm named after an English victory over Spain at Porto Bello in the Gulf of Mexico in 1739, it has developed over the past 50 years into a major antiques market. Traders, whether in the permanent shops or the Saturday stalls, are sharper than they may seem, and the only certain bargain is a lively atmosphere.

The road actually accommodates three markets. The antiques market, at the south end (Sat 6am–5pm), elides into a food market where the traditional fruit and vegetable stalls have been joined by traders selling fish, cheese and more exotic foodstuffs from around the world (Mon–Sat 9.30am–6pm, early closing Thurs 1pm). Next, a flea market mixing genuine junk with cutting-edge fashion operates under the Westway flyover, at the north end, on Fridays, Saturdays and Sundays.

As a backdrop to the food stalls, the refurbished **Electric Cinema** is London's oldest surviving movie house, dating from 1905. Just off Portobello Road, on Blenheim Crescent, is the **Travel Bookshop**, setting for the 1999 romantic comedy *Notting Hill*, in which Hugh Grant improbably wooed Julia Roberts. The film was based in the area principally because its writer, Richard Curtis, happened – like many media people – to live there. What the film didn't convey is the fact that Notting Hill is a melting pot in which several races and just about every social class rub shoulders. Grand, expensive Georgian townhouses at the Holland Park end contrast with their run-down counterparts a short distance northwards, where they are divided into bed-sits.

The main north-south artery, **Ladbroke Grove**, is the parade route for the **Notting Hill Carnival**, a massive three-day Caribbean festival which takes over the area in the last weekend of August,

Star attraction
● Portobello market

👁 **'Rural' Notting Hill**
In the 1840s James Weller Ladbroke tried to combine town and city environments by building squares and crescents of houses for the new wealthy around spacious gardens. These remain sought-after.

Below and Bottom: looking for bargains in Portobello Market

Map on page 80

Bird sanctuary
In the suburb of Barnes, between central London and Kew, is a magnet for birdwatchers, the WWT Wetland Centre (Queen Elizabeth's Walk, SW13, tel: 8409 4400, www.wetlandcentre.org.uk). Run by the Wildfowl & Wetlands Trust, it is a jigsaw of ponds, grasslands and mudflats, and has two imaginative exhibition areas.

with children's parades on the Sunday and adults' parades on Monday. It was started in 1966 in an attempt to unite the local communities after appalling race riots in the streets the previous year.

Westbourne Grove runs east to intersect with **Queensway**. Both have a continental flavour, with immigrants from Germany, Italy, Greece and the Middle East, and are packed with eating places.

WIMBLEDON

This southwest suburb hosts Britain's top tennis tournament in June/July and its history is captured in the **Wimbledon Lawn Tennis Museum** (The All-England Lawn Tennis & Croquet Club, Church Road, Wimbledon, tel: 8946 6131). The collection is a rich one, ranging from Victorian tableaux to Bjorn Borg's racket. Guided tours of the grounds can be booked but are expensive.

On the edge of Wimbledon Common, a large partly wooded expanse with nature trails, is the **Wimbledon Windmill Museum** (tel: 8947 2825, Apr–Oct Sat 2– 5pm, Sun 11am–5pm). The mill ended its working life in 1864. Today models and displays vividly illustrate the milling process.

Deer in Richmond Park

RICHMOND

Richmond Park and Kew Gardens are classic days out for Londoners, reached easily by District Line underground or by British Rail from Waterloo. The main attraction of Richmond is **Richmond Park**, at 2,350 acres (950 hectares) the largest of the royal parks, grazed by herds of red and fallow deer who enjoy the bracken thickets and gather beneath the dappled canopies of huge oaks. The park is also popular with horse riders. Rhododendrons and azaleas in May make the Isabella Plantation a particular high spot. The original royal residence in the park is the Palladian White Lodge (1727), now used by the Royal Ballet School.

Richmond Green is the handsome centre to the town, lined with 17th- and 18th-century buildings, and the remains of the 12th-century royal palace. Richmond Bridge is the oldest on the river, and the waterfront here is always lively: rowing boats can be hired.

Richmond Hill provides a grand view of the river. Below, reached along the towpath, is **Ham House** (Apr–Oct Sat–Wed 1–5pm; fee; tel: 8940 1950), a richly furnished 1610 Palladian building. The gardens, open all year, are a delight.

KEW

Kew, in the western suburbs of London, is synonymous with the ★★**Royal Botanic Gardens** (tel: 8332 1171, www.rbgkew.org.uk). The 300-acre (120-hectare) gardens were established in 1759 with the help of Joseph Banks, the botanist who named Botany Bay on Captain James Cook's first voyage to Australia. Other explorers and amateur enthusiasts added their specimens over the centuries, making this a formidable repository and research centre.

The gardens are also very beautiful, with grand glasshouses, including the Palm House and Water-lily House, Orangery, mock Chinese pagoda, and the 17th-century Dutch House, a former royal palace (currently undergoing major restoration). George III was locked up here when it was thought that he had gone mad. His wife Charlotte had a thatched summerhouse built in the grounds as a picnic spot. Two small art galleries focus on horticulture.

Star attraction
● **Kew Gardens**

Below: Ham House
Bottom: Kew's gardens

Map
on page
80

Estorick Collection

This remarkable collection of Italian Furturist art and other 20th-century masterpieces is housed in an elegant Georgian house in Islington (39A Canonbury Square, N1, tel: 7704 9522; Mon–Sat 11am–6pm, Sun 2–5pm). As well as Futurist paintings by Balla, Boccioni, Carrà, Severini and Russolo, there is some fine figurative art (1890–1950s) by Modigliani, Sironi, Campigli, de Chirico, Morandi and Marino Marini.

Islington antiques

17: North London

Islington – Camden – Hampstead – Highgate

ISLINGTON

This borough symbolises the new-style gentrification of London's Georgian and Victorian dwellings and a popular stereotype portrays it as the happy hunting ground of liberal-minded *bien pensants*. This is where Tony and Cherie Blair lived before moving to 10 Downing Street.

At the southern end of Islington, on Rosebery Avenue, which leads down to Holborn, stands **Sadler's Wells**, a 1,500-seat theatre built in 1683 and a principal ballet venue. The crossroads at the heart of Islington's shopping district is called the **Angel**, named after a long-gone coaching inn. Close by, towards the shops and eateries of Upper Street, is **Chapel Market**, a busy street market.

In nearby **Camden Passage**, the elegant buildings and arcades have become a treasure trove of antique shops, ranging from simple stalls to grand shops. Prices reflect the popularity of the place and it's hard to find great bargains.

Classic terraces can be found in squares such as **Canonbury Square**, where authors George Orwell and Evelyn Waugh once lived. At number 39A is the **Estorick Collection** *(see panel)*.

CAMDEN

It's **Camden Market** that attracts the crowds. The main market (Camden High Street, Thurs–Sun 9am–5.30pm) has cheap clothes. **Camden Lock Market** (off Chalk Farm Road, outdoor stalls Sat–Sun 10am–6pm, indoor stalls daily except Mon) concentrates on crafts. The quality of goods has fallen, even if the crowds haven't, and a nicer way to view Camden Lock is along one of the most attractive stretches of the ★**Regent's Canal**. This 8½-mile (14-km) stretch of water running from Paddington to West London to Limehouse in Docklands drops 86ft (25 metres) through 12 locks beneath 57 bridges. It is only about 4 ft (1.2 metres) deep, and in most places it is wide enough for two narrowboats to pass. To the east, near King's Cross, an old warehouse is now the **London Canal Museum** (12–13 New Wharf Road, tel: 7713 0836; closed Mon; fee), which graphically traces the ebb and flow of Britain's waterways.

A branch of the **Jewish Museum** (129–131 Albert Street, tel: 7284 1997; fee) tells the story of British Jewry and has a gallery devoted to Judaica. The other branch (at 80 East End Road, Finchley, tel: 8349 1143) depicts the migrations of Jews to London and has a Holocaust gallery.

HAMPSTEAD

Hampstead has long been a desirable address and especially attracts the successful literary set. Open spaces predominate. The 3 sq. mile (8 sq. km) **Heath** is the main 'green lung', leading down to **Parliament Hill** which gives splendid views across London, as does the 112-acre (45-hectare) **Primrose Hill** overlooking Regent's Park to the south. These are all welcome acres over which locals stride, walk dogs, fly kites, skate and swim in the segregated ponds. History-laden pubs include **Jack Straw's Castle**, the **Spaniards Inn** and the **Old Bull and Bush**.

★★**Kenwood House** (Hampstead Lane, tel: 8348 1286; daily 10am–6pm, Oct–Mar 10am–4pm; free), overlooking Hampstead Heath, looks like a great white wedding cake and showcases

Star attraction
● **Kenwood House**

Below: Hampstead village
Bottom: Camden Lock

Map on page 80

Below: memorial to Karl Marx in Highgate Cemetery
Bottom: Hampstead Heath

the **Iveagh Bequest**, a major art gallery with works by Rembrandt, Vermeer, Reynolds, Turner and Gainsborough. Poetry readings and chamber music recitals take place in the Orangery, and lakeside cocerts are held here in summer.

Sigmund Freud, fleeing the Nazis in 1938, moved from Vienna to 20 Maresfield Gardens, and his daughter Anna looked after it after his death a year later. The **Freud Museum** (tel: 7435 2002, Wed–Sun noon–5pm, fee) preserves the house as they left it. The original couch on which his Viennese patients free-associated is here.

The poet John Keats (1795–1821) wrote much of his work, including *Ode to a Nightingale*, during the two years he lived at Wentworth Place. The building, **Keats House** (tel: 7435 2062; May–Oct Tues–Sun noon–5pm) contains memorabilia such as his letters and a lock of his hair.

HIGHGATE

Neighbouring **Highgate,** a pleasant hill-top suburb built round a pretty square, contains London's grandest cemetery, where 300 famous people are buried. Consecrated in 1839, ★**Highgate Cemetery** (10am–5pm, 4pm in winter; fee) became fashionable. Besides its catacombs and impressive memorials, the attraction is the rather grim bust of Karl Marx, who was buried here in 1883.

18: East London

Hoxton – Bethnal Green – Spitalfields and Whitechapel – Docklands

East London was the first stop for many of the successive waves of immigrants whose labour helped fuel the Industrial Revolution and build the massive docks through which much of the British Empire's trade passed. Poverty and overcrowding were endemic. Although many areas remain poor, some have been gentrified.

HOXTON

The most recent such area is **Hoxton**, north of Old Street. The transformation began when young artists such as Damien Hirst and Tracey Emin moved there, many of them squatting in empty properties and creating studios in redundant warehouses and factories. As they became successful, art dealers and web designers followed and urban desolation became urban chic. Commercial galleries radiate from **Hoxton Square**, the location of Jay Jopling's fashionable White Cube2 gallery. Despite a rash of trendy café-bars and rising property prices that have forced out the less successful artists, the area still looks depressed.

A few minutes' walk to the northeast, on Kingsland Road, the ★ **Geffrye Museum** (tel: 7739 9893; Tues–Sat 10am–5pm, Sun noon– 5pm; free) is the only British museum to deal with the interior decorating tastes of the urban middle classes from 1600 to the present day. Originally intended to inspire workers in the East End furniture trade, it is a fascinating social chronicle.

BETHNAL GREEN

Once London's poorest area, Bethnal Green is home to the **National Museum of Childhood** (Cambridge Heath Road, tel: 8980 2415; closed Fri; free), a branch of the Victoria and Albert Museum. Displays range from classic children's toys (including some hands-on objects such as a rocking horse and model railways) to the

East and West
A traditional distinction was that London's West End had the money, the East End had the dirt; the West had leisure, the East labour.

Below: the White Cube2 art gallery in Hoxton
Bottom: an early 19th-century Regency room re-created at the Geffrye Museum

Map
on page
80

Below: Petticoat Lane market
Bottom: the drawing room
of Dennis Severs' house

development of nappies and the roots of adolescent rebellion. And there are some sobering facts about childcare and children's health.

Less than a mile away, the **Ragged School Museum** (46–50 Copperfield Road, E3, tel: 8980 6405; Wed–Thurs 10am–5pm) has a reconstructed kitchen and classroom to show how life was once lived by London's indomitable East Enders.

SPITALFIELDS AND WHITECHAPEL

The streets of **Spitalfields** contain several streets of architectural interest. These 18th-century houses were the homes of Huguenot silk weavers. With intricate porticos, large doors and shutters, many have been restored, and walking down **Fournier Street** at night you can see chandeliers lit in authentic, small, panelled rooms, with paintings on the walls and pewter plates on shelves. Most original is ★ **Dennis Severs' House** (18 Folgate Street, tel: 7247 4013; first Sun of month 2–5pm, first Mon of month noon–2pm; free), a four-storey town house still lit only by gaslight. The late Dennis Severs laid out the 10 rooms as if they were still being occupied by an 18th-century family; items such as a half-eaten scone contribute to this 'still-life drama'.

At the end of Fournier Street is **Christ Church**, completed in 1729 and considered the greatest of Nicholas Hawksmoor's churches.

To the west lies ★**Spitalfields Market**, a former wholesale fruit and vegetable market which now has a variety of antiques and crafts stalls during the week and organic food stalls on Sundays. To the south, in Middlesex Street, ★★**Petticoat Lane** market is packed with 1,000 stalls on Sundays, specialising in cheap clothes.

Responding to the East End's spiritual and economic poverty, a local vicar and his philanthropic wife founded the **Whitechapel Art Gallery** (Whitechapel High Street, tel: 7522 7861, Tues–Sun 11am–5pm, Wed until 8pm; free) in 1897. Lacking a permanent collection, it mounts high-profile exhibitions in a spectacular space. Picasso's *Guernica* was here in 1939.

To the south (just east of the Tower of London) is **St Katharine's Dock**. Built in 1828, it is now a pleasant yacht marina, with a variety of popular restaurants and pubs.

DOCKLANDS

London's docks, made derelict by heavy World War II bombing and rendered obsolete by the new container ports to the east, were transformed in the 1990s. Their proximity to the financial institutions of the City made them an attractive location for high-tech office buildings such as the 850-ft tall (260-metre) ★**Canary Wharf** complex. Several national newspapers have located their printing plants here.

It's worth taking a ride through the area on the **Docklands Light Railway** (from Bank to Greenwich) to see how property developers, encouraged by tax concessions and relaxed planning regulations, turned the place into an architectural adventure playground. Some find the variety intoxicating, others are repelled by the gigantic patchwork of glass, steel and concrete.

The ★**Museum in Docklands** (Number 1 Warehouse, West India Quay, tel: 7001 9800; fee) recounts 2,000 years of history. It includes a 20-ft (6-metre) model of Old London Bridge, complete with housing and shops, and there's a re-creation of the huge *Rhinebeck Panorama*, portraying a teeming Pool of London in 1810.

Star attraction
● **Petticoat Lane market**

Below: Canary Wharf's bulk, viewed from Greenwich
Bottom: Canary Wharf viewed from its Underground station

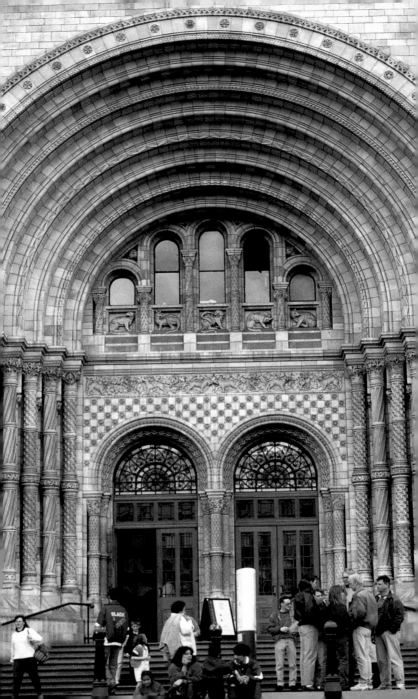

Architecture

TUDOR LONDON

A hallmark of the Renaissance buildings of Tudor times, often called 'Elizabethan' after Henry VIII's daughter Elizabeth I, is the use of half-timbering and red-brick. Staple Inn in High Holborn is a sole survivor from the period, while The George, a galleried coaching inn in Southwark's Borough High Street, though not built until 1687, would have been typical of this time.

ITALIAN CLASSICAL RENAISSANCE

Charles I brought a new elegance to the city in the shape of Inigo Jones (1573–1652). The court architect had travelled to Italy and he brought Italian Classical Renaissance to Britain in the fine Banqueting Hall in Whitehall Palace, and Queen Mary's House in Greenwich, both still standing, and the Palladian Covent Garden, set out, with the classic church of St Paul's, around London's first square.

WREN'S LONDON

Sir Christopher Wren (1632–1723) was a scientist and self-taught architect. His plans for the rebuilding of London after the Great Fire of 1666 were rejected, but he managed 52 churches (26 remain) as well as St Paul's Cathedral. Wren's mastery of harmonising baroque with classical design left its mark further afield, on the unimpeachable Greenwich and Chelsea naval and military hospitals, and on Kensington Palace.

GEORGIAN LONDON

John Nash (1752–1835) designed 50 elegant, formal villas in the classical style in what is now Regent's Park. He added great theatrical terraces, with Doric and Corinthian colonnades and sculpted pediments. The Adam brothers, two Scots who espoused 'Etruscan', planned Bedford Square, whose houses are typically Georgian: uninterrupted brick terraces with long sash windows and elaborated porticoes. A vogue for

> **Ancient London**
> Digging foundations for new office buildings in the City has unearthed many clues to the look of Roman London (1st–4th centuries) and Anglo-Saxon London (4th–10th centuries), and the Museum of London conveys some graphic impressions of the city's early life. The best example of Norman architecture (11th–12th centuries) is the Tower of London's White Tower. The oldest parts of Westminster Abbey are fine examples of Early Gothic ecclesiastical style (13th–15th centuries).

Opposite: entrance to the Natural History Museum
Below: Admiralty Arch

all things Greek followed: Sir Robert Smirke (1781–1867) modelled Covent Garden Theatre on the Temple of Minerva in Athens and designed the monumental British Museum.

THE VICTORIAN ERA

When the Old Palace of Westminster burned down in 1834, Augustus Pugin (1812–52) took the opportunity to lead a Gothic Revival with the new Houses of Parliament. Other examples include the main hall of the Royal Courts of Justice in Strand, St Pancras railway station in Euston Road, and Tower Bridge.

MODERN ARCHITECTURE

Conservatism dominates, but a mongrel medley of modern and post-modernist styles would include the spacious Royal Festival Hall (1951), the concrete bulk of the National Theatre (1967–77), the beehive-look Centre Point (1967), the US-style Broadgate office complex (1984), the futuristic Lloyd's of London (1986), Charing Cross Station (1990), the mammoth Canary Wharf complex in Docklands (1987 onwards), the 'glass testicle' or 'headlamp' of the GLA building (2002), the 'erotic gherkin' of the Swiss Reinsurance tower in the City (2003) and such elegantly airy stations on the Underground's Jubilee Line as Westminster and Canary Wharf.

Below: the Swiss Re building, nicknamed 'the gherkin', towers over traditional buildings in the City
Bottom: Houses of Parliament

Art Galleries

Bankside Gallery
48 Hopton Street, SE1. Tube: Blackfriars, Southwark; Tel: 7928 7521;
www.royalwatersociety.com

Home to the Royal Society of Painters in Watercolour and the Royal Society of Painter-Printmakers. Artists include David Cox, Russell Flint, John Singer Sargent, Auguste Rodin, Walter Sickert and Graham Sutherland.

Courtauld Gallery
Somerset House, The Strand, WC2. Tube: Temple. Tel: 7848 2645;
www.courtauld.ac.uk

The core collection contains key works by Impressionist and Post-Impressionist artists. Highlights: several notable works by Rubens, Seurat's *Young Woman Powdering Herself,* Renoir's *La Loge,* Cézanne's *Montagne Sainte-Victoire* (c.1887) and Manet's *Déjeuner sur l'herbe* (c.1863), a simplified replica of the painting now in the Musée d'Orsay, in Paris. Fee.

Dulwich Picture Gallery
Gallery Road, Dulwich Village, SE21. Rail: West Dulwich (from Victoria). Tel: 8693 5254;
www.dulwichpicturegallery.org.uk

The gallery, in a fine neoclassical building by Sir John Soane, is especially rich in 17th-century European painting and includes work by Claude, Cuyp, Hobbema, Rembrandt, Rubens, Van Dyck, Reni and Murillo. A highlight is seven paintings by Poussin, including *The Roman Road* and *Rainaldo and Armida. Sta Rita of Cascia.* Fee.

Guildhall Art Gallery
Guildhall Yard, EC2. Tube: Bank, St Paul's, Moorgate, Mansion House. Tel: 7606 3030;
www.guildhall-artgallery.org.uk

The gallery displays 250 paintings at a time from the Corporation of London's 4,000-strong collection. A selection of its best-known works are always on display, including Constable's *Salisbury Cathedral from the Meadows,* Edwin Landseer's *The First Leap,* John Everett Millais' *The Woodman's Daughter,* Frederic Leighton's

Special passes
Although national museums and galleries are free, most others charge for entry. Energetic visitors will benefit from the London Pass, which gives free entry to several dozen attractions and includes free travel on the Tube and buses. For latest prices, tel: 01664-500 107 or check www.londonpass.com

Joining the Art Fund, the UK's leading art charity, gives free admission to more than 200 museums, galleries and historic houses around the country, plus discounts on special exhibitions. For details, tel: 0870-848 2003 or check www. artfund.org

Gainsborough's 'Unknown Couple in a Landscape', Dulwich Picture Gallery

Buying pictures

The cluster of commercial galleries around Bond Street and Cork Street has been thinned out by rising rents, but a stroll from Oxford Circus to Green Park will reveal that many remain. You are not expected to buy in such galleries: they are shop windows, and selling often takes place behind the scenes, usually before an exhibition opens.

In recent years, the focus has moved eastwards to the area around Hoxton Square (see page 91). Dealers and fashionable galleries such as White Cube2 went there because many of the most promising younger artists were making studios for themselves in disused warehouses and factories in the East End. Rents have now risen and the next generation of young artists is likely to be have found affordable studios elsewhere.

Portraitist Sir Joshua Reynolds (1723–92), the first president of the Royal Academy

The Music Lesson and the gallery's popular Pre-Raphaelite paintings. Fee.

Hayward Gallery

South Bank Centre, Belvedere Road, SE1. Tube and rail: Waterloo. Tel: 7960 5226; www.hayward-gallery.org.uk

The Gallery shows a varied exhibition programme covering art, architecture and design. Its main programme includes monographic shows by international contemporary artists and thematic exhibitions. Fee.

National Gallery

Trafalgar Square, WC2. Tube: Charing Cross, Leicester Square. Tel: 7747 2885. www.national gallery.org.uk

This outstanding collection of Old Masters from the early Renaissance to 1900 includes *Bacchanal* by Poussin, *St Ursula* and *The Queen of Sheba* by landscape master Claude, paintings by Van Dyck, two admirable Rembrandts, a superb Aelbert Cuyp, Hogarth's *Six Pictures called Marriage à la Mode*, Titian's *Bacchus and Ariadne*, Rembrandt's *A Jew Merchant and Deposition*, Rubens' *Château de Steen*, Canaletto's *View of Venice* and Constable's *The Cornfield*. Free.

National Portrait Gallery

St Martin's Place, WC2. Tube: Charing Cross, Leicester Square. Tel: 7312 2463; www.npg.org.uk

This is the home of one of the world's strongest traditions of national portraiture. Since its beginnings in 1856, additions to the collection have been determined by the status of the sitter and historical importance of the portrait, not by their quality as works of art. Highlights include Holbein's large drawing of Henry VII and his son Henry VIII (*c.*1536–7), a life-like portrait of Queen Elizabeth I, sumptuous in brocade and pearls, and self-portraits of Hogarth, Gainsborough and Reynolds. Contemporary portraits include Martin Amis, Ewan McGregor, David Beckham and Tony Blair. Free.

Queen's Gallery

Buckingham Palace, Buckingham Palace Road, SW1. Tube: Green Park, Victoria, St

James's Park. Tel: 7839 1377. www.royal.gov.uk
The collection is predictably rich in royal portraits, notably by Holbein and Van Dyck. But there's much else, including three early Rembrandts, a Rubens self-portrait, 50 landscape paintings and 100 drawings by Canaletto, and an unrivalled collection of drawings by Da Vinci, Holbein, Raphael, Michelangelo, Poussin and Claude. Fee.

Royal Academy of Arts
Burlington House, Piccadilly, W1. Tube: Piccadilly Circus, Green Park. Tel: 7300 8000; www.royalacademy.org.uk
The RA, entered through a grand arch and across a large courtyard is well-known for high-profile temporary exhibitions. Its little-known permanent collection includes masterpieces such as Michelangelo's *Taddei Tondo*, Constable's *The Leaping Horse*, Gainsborough's *A Romantic Landscape* and Sargent's *Venetian Interior*. Diploma work, submitted by each Academician on election to membership, includes Walter Sickert's *Santa Maria Maggiore*, Stanley Spencer's *A Farm Gate* and David Hockney's *Grand Canyon*. Fee.

Tate Britain
Millbank, London SW1. Tube: Pimlico, Westminster. Tel: 7887 8000; www.tate.org.uk
This is the country's main gallery of British art. Highlights include Hogarth portraits, Constable's

Below: anonymous painting of Queen Elizabeth I from the National Portrait Gallery
Bottom: Claude Monet's 'The Thames below Westminster' in the National Gallery

Below: Dante Gabriel Rossetti's 'Beata Beatrix' in Tate Britain
Bottom: Sir Joshua Reynolds' 'Miss Jane Bowles' in the Wallace Collection

Flatford Mill, Millais' *Ophelia*, Stanley Spencer's *The Resurrection, Cookham* (1927), Francis Bacon's *Three studies for Figures at the Base of a Crucifixion*, and David Hockney's *Mr and Mrs Clark and Percy*. Among the British 20th-century sculptors represented are Jacob Epstein, Barbara Hepworth and Henry Moore. The Clore Gallery houses a magnificent collection of oil paintings and works on paper by Turner. Free.

Tate Modern
Bankside, London SE1. Tube: Southwark, Blackfriars, London Bridge. Tel: 7887 8000; www.tate.org.uk
Housed in a disused power station on the South Bank (easily reached from St Paul's Cathedral via the Millennium Bridge), this is Britain's most spectacular museum of modern and contemporary international art, big enough to absorb more than 5 million visitors a year. The old Turbine Hall hosts a succession of mammoth installations. Highlights in the themed galleries include Monet's *Water-Lilies*, Dalí's *Autumnal Cannibalism*, Sickert's *La Hollandaise,* Bonnard's *The Bath,* Joseph Beuys' *Untitled (Vitrine)*, Picasso's collage *Bottle of Vieux Marc, Glass, Guitar and Newspaper*, and Andy Warhol's *Electric Chair.* Free.

Wallace Collection
Hertford House, Manchester Square, W1. Tube: Bond Street, Baker Street. Tel: 7563 9500. www.the-wallace-collection.org.uk
The closed collection ranks among the most superb assembly of French art outside Paris. In addition to pictures by Watteau, Boucher and Fragonard, it contains Rembrandt's self-portrait *The Artist in a Cap*, Velazquez's *Lady with a Fan*, Rubens' *Rainbow Landscape*, Franz Hals's *Laughing Cavalier*, and Poussin's *Dance to the Music of Time*. Paintings from the English School include Reynolds' *Miss Jane Bowles* and *The Strawberry Girl*. The house also has an array of priceless furniture, porcelain and armour. Free.

● For comprehensive reviews of these and many lesser known galleries in the capital, see *Insight Guides: Museums and Galleries of London.*

Theatre & Music

London's theatrical history goes back to a playhouse opened at Shoreditch in 1576 by James Burbage, the son of a carpenter and travelling player. In modern times, live theatre was supposed to succumb first to movies, then to television, yet it is still one of those essential attractions that every visitor is expected to experience. It remains a mystery, however, what cultural sustenance coachloads of foreign tourists derive from a convoluted Alan Ayckbourn farce or an imaginative production of Shakespeare set in a variant of the Third Reich. More cautious visitors play it safe and opt for one of the blockbuster musicals.

Revenue from musicals could be used to underwrite more serious work. In particular, Trevor Nunn, who grew rich by directing Andrew Lloyd Webber musicals, including *Cats*, masterminded the Royal Shakespeare Company's 1985 production of *Les Misérables*. Despite a tepid critical welcome, 'Les Mis' triumphed, and Nunn became director of the National Theatre (the subsidsed three-theatre complex on the South Bank).

Stars remain important. Favourite thespians such as Michael Gambon, Maggie Smith and Judi Dench can virtually guarantee a full house. Also, Hollywood stars such as Kevin Spacey, Dustin Hoffman, Nicole Kidman and Gwyneth Paltrow

Half-price tickets
The 'tkts' booth in Leicester Square, run by the theatres themselves, sells same-day tickets for West End shows at up to 50 percent off, plus a £2.50 service fee (10am–7pm Mon–Sat, noon–3pm Sun). The National Theatre sells a limited number of full-price same-day tickets at 10am at its South Bank box office — useful when a show is sold out.

Advance tickets can be bought through agencies such as First Call (7420 0000) and Ticketmaster (7344 4444) at full price plus booking fee. To avoid the fee, you can buy directly from individual box offices.

Once more onto the barricades…

Behind the Scenes
The National Theatre runs an interesting back-stage tour, which imparts information and anecdote in equal measure: 'Why are the seats in the Olivier theatre lilac-coloured? Because that was Lord Olivier's favourite colour.' Timings and reservations: tel 7452 3400.

Below: ticket agency window
Bottom: the Royal Albert Hall

have taken stage roles in London, pulling in the crowds. In addition to the 50 central theatres staging classics and new works, around 60 fringe venues unveil experimental work.

MUSIC

Top concert venues include the **Royal Festival Hall** (South Bank, tel: 7960 4242), popular despite less than perfect acoustics; the **Barbican Centre** (Silk Street, tel: 7638 8891), home of the London Symphony Orchestra; the **Royal Albert Hall** (Kensington Gore, tel: 7589 8212), also acoustically challenged, hosts the summer series of BBC Promenade Concerts (the 'Proms'); and the **Wigmore Hall** (36 Wigmore Street, tel: 7935 2141 has both excellent acoustics and renowned chamber recitals. Lunchtime concerts are held at several churches: **St John's, Smith Square** (Westminster, tel: 7222 1061), **St Martin-in-the-Fields** (Trafalgar Square, tel: 7930 0089) and **St Mary-le-Bow** (Cheapside, tel: 7248 5139).

Top jazz venues include **Ronnie Scott's** (47 Frith Street, tel: 7439 0747), **Jazz Café** (5 Parkway, Camden, tel: 7916 6060) and **Pizza Express Jazz Club** (10 Dean Street, Soho, tel: 7439 8722).

The popularity of rock venues waxes and wanes. The latest shows are comprehensively covered in *Time Out* magazine and in the *Evening Standard*'s Thursday listings magazine.

London for Families

These 20 attractions are popular with children, though not all will suit every age group.

❶ **London Zoo**. Animals and birds from around the world. *See page 57.*

❷ **London Aquarium**. Fish from around the world. *See page 22.*

❸ **London Eye**. A ride on the world's biggest observation wheel. *See page 23.*

❹ **Science Museum**. From early steam engines to modern spacecraft. *See page 51.*

❺ **Natural History Museum**. From dinosaurs to creepy-crawlies. *See page 50.*

❻ **Madame Tussaud's**. As close as most will get to their heroes. *See page 58.*

❼ **London Dungeon**. For kids who prefer their history gory and grisly. *See page 74.*

❽ **Funland**. The latest games at the Trocadero Centre, Piccadilly. *See page 34.*

❾ **National Museum of Childhood**. How kids have lived and played. *See page 91.*

❿ **Hamleys**. Where to buy the toys of today. *See page 43.*

⓫ **London Transport Museum**. Trams, trains and buses, well presented. *See page 31.*

⓬ **Theatre Museum**. A chance to dress up as Lady Capulet or a mouse. *See page 32.*

⓭ **Golden Hinde**. What life was like on Drake's 16th-century sailing ship. *See page 76.*

⓮ **HMS Belfast**. What life was like on a World War II warship. *See page 73.*

⓯ **Imperial War Museum**. See tanks, cannon and fighter planes close up. *See page 78.*

⓰ **Firepower**. Artillery simulators show what it's like to be a gunner. *See page 84.*

⓱ **Winston Churchill's Britain at War Experience**. Live as it was lived in London in the early 1940s. *See page 74.*

⓲ **St James's Park**. A peaceful place to feed the ducks. *See page 41.*

⓳ **Battersea Park**. Adventure playground, boating lake and deer. *See page 55.*

⓴ **Coram Fields**. Paddling pool, grazing farm animals and café. *See page 59.*

Below: David Beckham and England football manager Sven-Goran Eriksson at Madame Tussaud's – can you tell they're made of wax? Bottom: an exhibit from the National Museum of Childhood

FOOD AND DRINK

London is one of the great culinary cities of the world. This is partly due to the sheer breadth of cosmopolitan cuisines available and also the fact that there has been a re-evaluation of the indigenous cuisine of the British. Its once scorned reputation of badly cooked, unimaginative, stodgy meals has been overturned by the new generation of innovative British chefs.

They have injected new life into traditional English recipes – indeed rediscovering many – by combining them with French and ethnic influences. They take pride in making the best of top quality and seasonal ingredients whilst also making meals lighter. For example, dishes such as 'roast best end of lamb with two sauces of lime and coriander, yoghurt and mint' or 'courgette flowers with lobster mousseline and a caviar butter sauce'.

It's still a frequent complaint, though, that eating out in London is too rarely good value for money. This is partly because high rents and other overheads push up prices, and partly because the fast expansion of the restaurant culture has exceeded the supply of good chefs.

The main concentration of restaurants is to be found in the West End, with Soho providing the most interesting and widest choice, whilst Covent Garden offers good value pre-theatre suppers. Other concentrations can be found in Kensington, Chelsea and Notting Hill. The City, with its oyster bars and restaurants traditionally catering for the business luncher, becomes a ghost town in the evenings and at weekends.

Although London's restaurants are expensive by many people's standards, reflecting the high cost of living, eating out in this capital has arguably never been so good. Ethnic restaurants – especially Indian – provide some of the best-value meals in town, whereas pubs and wine bars often provide good inexpensive snacks in surroundings that are preferable to a fast-food hamburger joint.

Roast beef: The great traditions of Sunday lunch and roast carveries are still very much alive and sampling them provides an insight into everyday life in England. However, choose carefully, as there is a huge difference between good and bad versions of these meals. Even the 1996 'mad cow disease' scare didn't kill demand for roast beef – although some chefs found other European sources for their meat.

Traditional fish and chips: It's surprisingly hard to find this nutritious British dish cooked freshly to order (as opposed to reheated), but the real thing can be found at Rock & Sole Plaice (47 Endell Street, Covent Garden), Sea Shell (49–51 Lisson Grove, Marylebone) and Geales (2 Farmer Street, Notting Hill).

Afternoon tea

This traditional genteel event takes place in some of the grander hotels at around 3.30pm and consists of thinly-cut sandwiches (often cucumber), a variety of cakes and a pot of tea. The brew varies from classic Indian teas such as Assam and Darjeeling to the more flowery Earl Grey. Venues include Palm Court, Waldorf Astoria, Aldwych, WC2 (tel: 7836 2400), which also has tea dances; the Ritz, Piccadilly, W1 (tel: 7493 8181 and book well ahead); Brown's, 21–24 Albemarle Street, W1 (tel: 7493 6020); the Savoy (Strand, WC2, tel: 7836 4343) and the Dorchester (Park Lane, W1 (tel: 7629 8888).

Opposite: lunching in Covent Garden

Tipping: Check on the menu when ordering whether a service charge is automatically added to the bill – it usually is, at 10 or 12.5 per cent. Even then, many restaurants will slyly leave the gratuities space blank on your credit card slip in the hope that you'll add a further tip. Don't.

PUBS

Like most other things in a city this size, it is impossible to generalise about the 5,000-plus pubs in London. Some have live music, some stage striptease, some are genteel and some rough, many are Victorian and some were opened last week, perhaps part of a youth-oriented chain such as The Slug and Lettuce. Most Londoners have a favourite, the choice of which depends as much on the people that frequent it as on the decor.

London has several pubs that date from the 17th century, and many retain the atmosphere of that era. One of the best examples is The George in Southwark's Borough High Street, the only surviving galleried coaching inn in London and now owned by the National Trust. A fine example of the explosion of pubs during the Victorian era (known for their engraved mirrors, grand central bars and dark velvet

---

Coffee wars

Coffee shops are nothing new in London. The first 'coffee house' was set up in 1652 and they spread rapidly as places where merchants, brokers, lawyers and politicians could meet to do business. By the end of the century there were 2,000 of them. In the late 1950s, coffee bars in Soho nourished pioneering rock singers such as Tommy Steele. The 21st century began with a massive expansion by Starbucks, closely followed by other chains such as Coffee Republic, Costa, Caffè Nero and various internet cafés. *Plus ça change…*

---

upholstery) is the Duke of Cumberland in Fulham, where such decor is completed by Grecian urns.

The traditional drink in a pub is English beer (ale or bitter). The genuine article is drawn up by hand pump and served at the temperature of the cellar; chilling literally kills it, as beer continues to ferment in the barrel. A lager is closest to Continental and American beers, a stout is a dark, strong beer (such as Guinness), but most seasoned British drinkers prefer bitter, a light brown beer that should taste fresh, hoppy, with no fizzy gas and is served at room temperature.

A pint is just over half a litre and many people order a 'half', instead of a full pint. In traditional pubs, customers orders their drinks at the bar and pay for them immediately. It is not necessary to tip.

Chains such as All Bar One and the Slug and Lettuce are a growing presence. These light, airy, fashionably furnished pub/bars are especially accessible to single drinkers, women and anyone wanting a quiet drink during the daytime. Many offer imaginative modern menus.

Most traditional pubs also serve food, although probably not all day. 'Pub grub' generally refers to food bought over the bar rather than an elaborate restaurant-style meal. The menus available at lunchtime generally provide good value and often include traditional British dishes. Bangers and mash (sausages and mashed potato, often accompanied by fried onions), bubble and squeak (a mixture of fried cabbage, onions and potato, often served with cold meat), Ploughman's lunch (Cheddar cheese, bread and mixed pickles), steak and kidney pie or pudding, and sausage rolls are all traditional pub fare, although many pubs now offer more adventurous food, with Mediterranean influences.

Restaurants selection

Prices indicate the cost of a three-course evening meal for two with a bottle of house wine, but do not include coffee or service.

£££ = expensive (£50-plus)
££ = moderate (£30–50)
£ = inexpensive (under £30)

● For a comprehensive selection of the city's restaurants, consult Insight Guides' 176-page *Eating in London*.

TRADITIONAL BRITISH

Boisdale. 15 Eccleston Street, SW1 (tel: 7730 6922). A Scottish flavour and a vast selection of whiskies. **££**.

Fortnum and Mason, St James's Restaurant. 4th floor, 181 Piccadilly, W1. Tel: 7734 8040. Good English food, as you would expect from a restaurant located within this famous food emporium. Not overpriced, it serves traditional cooked breakfasts and excellent roast lunches, as well as afternoon and high teas. **££**.

Greens Restaurant & Oyster Bar. 36 Duke Street, SW1. Tel: 7930 4566. There is a clubby, English atmosphere served up with solid British food in the heart of St James's. **£££**.

The Quality Chop House. 94 Farringdon Road, EC1. Tel: 7837 5093. A 19th-century city clerks' dining room with its original interior of fixed wooden seating still intact. The food, however, is up-market with the likes of blue fish with fennel sauce on the menu beside plain lamb chops. **££**.

The Ritz, Louis XVI Restaurant Piccadilly, W1. Tel: 7493 8181. Elegant Edwardian restaurant decorated in Louis XVI style. The dining room is sumptuous but some say that the food could be better value. Jacket and tie dress code. **£££**.

Rules. 35 Maiden Lane, WC2. Tel: 7836 5314/379 0258. Exceptionally good for English game such as grouse, wild salmon, Highland roe deer and wild boar, when in season. Does a good roast beef, traditional puddings and real ale. **£££**.

St John. 26 St John St, EC1. Tel: 7251 0848. The meat and offal-heavy menu offers unusual pairings such as Middle-white belly and dandelion, rabbit and lentils, goose and watercress, and roast bone marrow and parsley salad. **££££**

Simpsons-in-the-Strand. 100 Strand, WC2. Tel: 7836 9112. The Grand Divan Tavern is an Edwardian dining room renowned for London's best roast beef. Staunchly traditional and formal. **£££**.

Tate Britain Restaurant. The Tate Britain, Millbank, SW1. Tel: 7887 8825. Beautifully decorated with Rex Whistler's mural, this fine lunch restaurant has a excellent wine list. **££**.

MODERN EUROPEAN

Alastair Little. 49 Frith Street, W1. Tel: 7734 5183. The chef-owner has an inventive approach to food in a basic French mode. Delicious, fresh, nouvelle-style cooking. Trendy, stark retro-1980s decor. Booking essential. **£££**.

Bibendum. Michelin House, 81 Fulham Road, SW3. Tel: 7581 5817. Set in this beautifully modernised Art Nouveau building, this is a landmark restaurant in more ways than one. The cuisine is a modern fusion of styles and flavours and the service is impressive. So are the prices. **£££**.

Bluebird. 350 King's Road, SW3. Tel: 7559 1000. Conran's European/Pacific Rim fusion restaurant in Chelsea. The place is noisy and glamorous and the food innovative. **£££**.

L'Escargot. 48 Greek Street, W1. Tel: 7437 2679. Ever fashionable landmark in Soho which remains popular with the theatrical and media crowd. Restaurant upstairs and a brasserie on the ground floor. Modern English and French cuisine. First-class wine list. **£££**.

The Ivy. 1 West Street, WC2. Tel: 7836 4751. Popular media and celebrity haunt, with high-quality decor, gallery-worthy art, well thought-out food and possibly the presence of a few Hollywood stars. Booking is essential. **£££**.

Kensington Place. 201 Kensington Church Street, W8. Tel: 7727 3184. Fashionable and informal, this New York-style restaurant is always bustling. The decor is modernist, while the food is fairly conservative in style. **£££**.

Orrery. 55 Marylebone High Street, W1 (tel: 7616 8000). One of Terence Conran's more lauded enterprises. **£££**.

Oxo Tower. Wharf, Barge House Street, SE1. Tel: 7803 3888. Brasserie and restaurant run by Harvey Nichols. Main attraction is the stunning river view. **£££**.

People's Palace. Royal Festival Hall, SE1 (tel: 7928 9999). Spacious restaurant with great views over the Thames. Less busy mid-evening during RFH concerts. **££**

Le Pont de la Tour. Butlers Wharf Building, 36D Shad Thames, SE1. Tel: 7403 8403. Chic Conran restaurant with superb Thames views. The fixed price menus are a bargain for this level of cuisine; otherwise it's quality at a price. **£££**.

The Portrait. National Portrait Gallery, St Martin's Place, WC2. Tel: 7312 2490. This top-floor restaurant offers great views of Nelson's Column in the pedestrianised Trafalgar Square and Big Ben. And the food is above average by most gallery restaurant standards. **£££**

Quaglino's. 16 Bury Street, SW1. Tel: 7930 6767. Located in a basement that was once a ballroom, this huge Terence Conran enterprise reproduces the buzz of 1930s London, with a wide menu. **£££**.

Tuttons. 11–12 Russell St, WC]. Tel: 7836 4141. Aside from the merits of its Covent Garden position, this is a fun place for brunch or lunch, with some nice variations on brasserie fare. For a tourist venue, it's surprisingly good. **£££**

FRENCH

Le Café Des Amis. 11–14 Hanover Place, WC2. Tel: 7379 3444. Always crowded, largely due to its Covent Garden position and reliable French food with an international flavour. Typical French brasserie menu and efficient service. Bar downstairs and Salon upstairs. There's no obligation to eat a full meal. **££**.

Le Caprice. Arlington House, Arlington Street, SW1. Tel: 7629 2239. Black and white café-style restaurant that is a fashionable place to graze and be seen. Pianist in the evenings. Excellent New York style Sunday brunch. **£££**.

Chez Gérard. 8 Charlotte Street, W1. Tel: 7636 4975. Especially good for meat, this French bistro serves excellent steak and chips. Also good traditional cooking such as *soupe de poisson* and Chateaubriand. Pleasant simple French decor. **££**.

Le Gavroche. 43 Upper Brook Street, W1. Tel: 7408 0881. The excellence of Albert Roux made this the first British restaurant to earn three Michelin stars. Very expensive. Set lunch is best value. **£££**.

Gordon Ramsay. 68–69 Royal Hospital Road, SW3. Tel: 7352 4441. A luxurious setting for the Michelin-starred chef's interpretation of classic French cuisine. Genuine haute cuisine and a true gastronomic experience. The set lunch is good value; à la carte is pricey. **£££**.

Langan's Brasserie. Stratton Street, W1. Tel: 7491 8822. Langan's reputation for attracting celebrities often overshadows the notable food. British actor Michael Caine is part-owner of this continually fashionable brasserie. **£££**.

Odins. 27 Devonshire Street, W1. Tel: 7935 7296. Glamorous and richly adorned with paintings by the likes of David Hockney. Delicate food with traditional English and French influences. **£££**.

GREEK

Elysée. 13 Percy St, W1. Tel: 7636 4804. Live music and cabarets with belly dancer accompany the prawn cocktails, kleftico, taramasalata and steak Diane. Note that Zorba-like plate breaking is chargeable. **££–£££**

The Real Greek. 15 Hoxton Market, N1. Tel: 7739 8212. Imaginative fare in fashionable location that featured in the movie *Bridget Jones's Diary*. **££**.

ITALIAN

Bertorelli's. 44A Floral Street, WC2. Tel: 7836 3969. Black and white Art Deco style restaurant that has become something of an institution in Covent Garden. Serves reliable modern Italian food. **££**.

Café Venezia. 15–16 New Burlington Street, W1. Tel: 7439 2378. Informal restaurant serving home-made pasta. **££**.

Cibo. 3 Russell Gardens, W14. Tel: 7371 6271. Comfortable and airy with intriguing art on the walls, modern northern Italian cooking. **££**.

Orso. 27 Wellington Street, WC2. Tel: 7240 5269. Set in a basement with simple decor, authentic north Italian food and good service. Fashionable with actors and theatregoers alike. **£££**.

Rocket. 4–5 Lancashire Court, W1. Tel: 7629 2889. Lively, simply decorated modern Italian with a menu of 12-inch wood-fired pizzas, pasta and salad in a pretty enclave just off New Bond Street. Arrive early for a seat outside. **££**..

San Lorenzo. 22 Beauchamp Place, SW3. Tel: 7584 1074. Fashionable and busy posh Knightsbridge restaurant. The menu is a mixture of the exciting and the mundane. Extraordinary decor incorporates a sliding roof for summer. **£££**.

The River Café. Thames Wharf, Rainville Road, W6. Tel: 7381 8824. By the Thames near Hammersmith, designed by the prominent architect Richard Rogers and run by his wife. Delightful northern Italian food and riverside tables. **£££**.

CHINESE

China City. White Bear Yard, 25A Lisle Street, WC2. Tel: 7734 3388. Traditional Chinese food served in a tranquil setting. Two spacious, airy rooms overlook a courtyard with a fountain. An oasis of calm amid the central London bustle. **££**.

Chuen Cheng Ku. 17 Wardour Street, W1. Tel: 7437 1398. Huge, functional place that has a reputation for serving some of the best dim sum in town (until 6pm). Popular with locals at lunch time. **££**.

Fung Shing. 15 Lisle Street, WC2. Tel: 7437 1539. Has long been one of the best Chinatown restaurants and consequently is always packed. Some original dishes with particularly good fish. **££**.

Harbour City. 46 Gerrard St, W1. Tel: 7439 7859. This is an excellent, reasonably priced restaurant in the middle of Chinatown. Dim sum (served Mon–Sat until 5pm) dominates the menu with some interesting variations. **££**

Memories of China. 67 Ebury Street, SW1. Tel: 7730 7734. The late Ken Lo, renowned Chinese cookery writer, started up this classy restaurant where dishes originate from the many regions of China and standards are high. **£££**.

Poon's. 4 Leicester Street, W1. Tel: 7437 1528. The best of several branches of Poon in Central London. Wind-dried meats are a distinctive feature on the long menu of more than 200 dishes. Good value. **££**.

Royal China. 13 Queensway, W2.Tel: 7221 2535. The ambience is nothing special, but the menu is first-rate, offering superb dim sum, delicious lobster with noodles, and delicate spring rolls. **££**

INDIAN

Bombay Brasserie. Bailey's Hotel, Courtfield Close, SW7. Tel: 7370 4040. The stylish decor harks back to the days of the Raj. There are dishes from many regions. Lunch-time buffet is good value. **£££**.

Khan's. 13 Westbourne Grove, W2. Tel: 7727 5420. This huge Indian dining room is famous for being great value. Crowded in the evenings, the atmosphere is that of constant hustle and bustle. **££**.

Last Days of the Raj. 22 Drury Lane, WC2. Tel: 7836 1628. One of London's most respected Indian restaurants, good for Bengali dishes. **££**.

The Red Fort. 77 Dean Street, W1. Tel: 7437 2115. Renowned Soho restaurant with good Mogul cooking in luxurious surroundings. Its creator, Amin Ali, has produced a stylish setting and the restaurant is noted for its interesting menu. **£££**.

Veeraswamy. Victory House, 101 Regent St, W1. Tel: 7734 1401. London's oldest Indian eatery. Elegant, colonial style. **£££**.

Zaika. 1 Kensingston High St, W8. Tel: 7795 6533. Situated in a converted high-street bank, Zaika has a stylish and luxurious feel. Chef Vineet Bhatia turns out fragrant and subtle dishes. The coconut soup and grilled lobster tail with spiced lobster jus is a taste sensation. Good-value set lunch menu. **£££–££££**

JAPANESE

Ikeda. 30 Brook Street, W1. Tel: 7629 2730. Sit at the Yakitori and Sushi bars to get the best Japanese experience at this fashionable Mayfair restaurant. **£££**.

Ikkyu. 67 Tottenham Court Road, W1. Tel: 7636 9280. Relaxed basement restaurant with good value, quality food and less of the usual Japanese emphasis on decor and service. Large Japanese following. **££**.

Nobu. Metropolitan Hotel, 19 Old Park Lane, W1. Tel: 7447 4747. Inventive cooking and celebrated cocktails. **£££**.

Yo Sushi. 52 Poland Street W1. Tel: 7287 0443. Fun eating, with robot service and what's claimed to be the longest conveyor belt service in the world. **£**.

Wagamama. 101A Wigmore Street, W1. Tel: 7409 0111. Minimalist fast food noo-dle restaurant. Good fresh interesting Japanese food at reasonable prices. Branches also in Jamestown Road NW1 and Lexington Street W1. **£**.

Zuma. 5 Raphael St, SW7. Tel: 7584 1010. An large menu includes excellent sushi and sashimi, delicious skewers from the robata grill, and 22 varieties of sake. This is A-list territory and reservations are needed well in advance. **££££**

OTHER ETHNIC EATERIES

Calabash. 38 King Street, WC2. Tel: 7836 1976. Situated below the Africa Centre close to Covent Garden Piazza with dishes from many regions of the African continent. Coffee is particularly good. Also African wine and beer. **££**.

Fakhreldine. 85 Piccadilly, W1. Tel: 7493 3424. Overlooking Green Park, this is one of London's smartest and most established Lebanese restaurants. **£££**.

Gay Hussar. 2 Greek Street, W1. Tel: 7437 0973. A long menu of mouth-watering dishes, such as wild cherry soup, keep this fine established Hungarian restaurant very popular. Value for money. **£££**.

Momo's. Second Floor, Selfridges, 400 Oxford St, W1. Tel: 7318 3620. This offers foot-sore shoppers a light mezze menu in relaxed surroundings. Or you can stop off for a refreshing mint tea in the luxurious tearoom. **££–£££**

Souk. 27 Litchfield St, WC2. Tel: 7240 1796. Cramped but decidedly atmospheric, it's the perfect setting for a Moroccan feast. The menu offers the usual mezze for starters, with a selection of couscous and tagine dishes for the main. **££**

FISH

Geales. 2-4 Farmer Street, W8. Tel: 7727 7528. Busy fish restaurant at Notting Hill Gate. Good fish and chips cooked in beef dripping. **££**.

Live Bait. 43 The Cut, SE1. Tel: 7928 7211. Also at 21 Wellington Street, WC2. Tel: 7836 7161. Good shellfish and imaginatively presented fish dishes. **£££**.

Ancient eateries

There is some evidence that the Romans ran a public kitchen in London 2,000 years ago, but the first known restaurant was a 'public place of cookery' recorded by a 12th-century monk. Situated by the Thames, it included different dining areas for the rich and poor and was probably large enough not to be daunted by the prospect of feeding passing armies. Eating houses multiplied in the 14th and 15th centuries, with the price of meals regulated by the authorities. It was possible to bring along your own food and have it cooked for you. In the 18th century, 'chop houses' were the precursors of modern restaurants.

Fish! Cathedral Street, close to Borough Market, SE1. Tel: 7836 3236. Noisy place in shadow of Southwark Cathedral, serving fresh fish in simple dishes. **££**.

Rudland & Stubbs. 35–37 Greenhill Rents, Cowcross Street, EC1. Tel: 7253 0148. English and French-style fish dishes in a characterful setting with tiled walls and raw floor boards, around the corner from Smithfield Meat Market. **££**.

Sheekey's. 28–32 St Martin's Court, WC2. Tel: 7240 2565. Edwardian fish restaurant which reflects its theatrical surroundings. The menu includes traditional potted shrimps, fish pies and eels and mash at somewhat high prices. **£££**.

Sweetings. 39 Queen Victoria Street, EC4. Tel: 7248 3062. Beautiful interior of tiles and mosaics add to the atmosphere of this busy, traditonal City hang out. Varied menu which includes potted shrimps and stodgy English puddings. **£££**.

Wheelers. 12A Duke of York Street, WC2. Tel: 7930 2460. The chain's flagwhip restaurant in St James's, renovated by celebrity chef Marco Pierre White. **£££**.

VEGETARIAN

Eat and Two Veg. 50 Marylebone High St, W1. Tel: 7258 8595. Welcome newcomer to the Marylebone scene, this formica and leatherette diner serves creative vegetarian concoctions. **££**

Food For Thought. 31 Neal Street, WC2. Tel: 0171-836 0239. Small and crowded at lunch times, with queues for take-aways. The food is never dull. Bring your own wine. Dinner served until 8.30pm. **£**.

The Gate. 51 Queen Caroline Street, W6 (tel: 8748 6932). Highly regarded Hammersmith restaurant. **££**

Mildred's. 58 Greek Street, W1. Tel: 7494 1638. Imaginative cooking put together in cafe-style surroundings. Vegan options. **£**.

LATE-NIGHT EATING

Borshtch 'n' Tears. 46 Beauchamp Place, SW3. Tel: 7584 9911. Last orders 2am. Zany Russian restaurant.. The inexpensive menu includes delicacies such as blinis and caviar, chicken kiev, golubtsy and Siberian Pilmenni. **££**.

Costa Dorada. 47–55 Hanway St, W1. Tel: 7636 7139. Last orders 2.30am. This lively restaurant/ tapas bar with a strong Spanish following fills up in the late evening when diners flock in for the colourful flamenco dancing and live Spanish music. **£££**.

Joe Allen. 13 Exeter Street, WC2. Tel: 020 7836 0651. Last orders 12.45am. Fashionable American restaurant hidden down an alley in Covent Garden. Largely patronised by those involved with the media and showbiz. Booking essential. **££**.

Maroush II. 38 Beauchamp Place, SW3. Tel: 7581 5434. Last orders 2am. Largely patronised by nocturnal Middle Easterners. The food, which includes Lebanese delicacies such as sujuk (spicy sausages) and shish taouk (cubes of chicken charcoal grilled), is well presented. **£££**.

Mr Kong. 21 Lisle St WC2. Tel: 7437 7341. Last orders 2am. Renowned for great seafood and lack of decor. **££**.

Pick of the pubs

TRADITIONAL PUBS

Anchor. 1 Bankside, SE1. 18th-century riverside pub where Dr Johnson hung out. Several small bars plus outside tables.

Angel. 21 Rotherhithe Street, SE16. A 15th-century pub built on stilts over the Thames. Good views of Tower Bridge.

Black Friar. 174 Queen Victoria Street, EC4. Art nouveau exterior and marbled interior with bronze friezes of monks.

Coach and Horses. 29 Greek Street, W1. Attracts creative types, serious drinkers trying to prolong Soho's bohemian past.

Fox & Anchor. 115 Charterhouse Street, EC1. City pub near Smithfield meat market famous for huge English breakfasts.

George Inn. 77 Borough High Street, SE1. London's only surviving galleried inn, once used by stagecoaches and now owned by the National Trust. Crowded.

Grapes. 76 Narrow Street, E14. Riverside deck, Dickensian atmosphere. Mobile phones banned. Good fish and chips.

Grenadier. Old Barrack Yard, 18 Wilton Row, SW1. Real gem hidden away in quiet cobbled mews.

The Guinea. 30 Bruton Place, SW1. Excellent English food such as steak and kidney pie in a pub setting.

Jerusalem Tavern. 55 Britton Street, EC1. An 18th-century Farringdon pub with wide range of exotic beers and no music.

Lamb. 94 Lamb's Conduit Street, WC1. Fine Victorian restoration, good beer.

Prospect of Whitby. 57 Wapping Wall, E1. Dates to 1520. Many authentic original touches but many tourists too.

Red Lion. 48 Parliament Street, SW1, One of the few pubs close to Westminster and frequented by parliamentarians.

Spaniards Inn. Hampstead Lane, NW3. Dtaes to 16th century and reputed to have been used by highwayman Dick Turpin.

Trafalgar Tavern. Park Row, Greenwich, SE10. Built in 1837 in honour of Admiral Horatio Nelson. Riverside terrace.

Ye Olde Cheshire Cheese. 145 Fleet Street, EC4. Maze of small bars. Known to Dr Johnson and Charles Dickens.

👁 Eating out

London's climate and traffic fumes don't make it the ideal city for pavement cafés. But here are some pleasant venues for al fresco dining, when conditions permit.

- **Aquarium.** Ivory House, St Katharine-by-the-Tower, E1. Relaxing waterside terrace.
- **Carluccio's Caffè.** 3–5 Barrett Street, W1. Italian deli near Oxford Street's shopping.
- **Engineer.** 65 Gloucester Avenue, NW1. Primrose Hill pub with large garden.
- **Kew Greenhouse.** 1 Station Parade, TW9. Large terrace, emphasis on organic food.
- **Troubadour.** 265 Old Brompton Road, SW5. Bohemian coffee house.
- **Tuttons.** 11–12 Russell Street, WC2. Covent Garden brasserie. Can get crowded.

GAY PUBS

Soho, London's traditional bohemian centre, has more than a dozen gay venues, but most areas with nightlife will have at least one bar where gays tend to meet.

Admiral Duncan, 54 Old Compton Street, W1. Traditional pub in the heart of Soho's gay scene. More mature patrons.

Candy Bar. 23–24 Bateman Street, W1. Soho's leading lesbian bar. Late opening; admission charge after 9pm Fri, Sat.

Retro Bar. 2 George Court, off Strand, WC2. More relaxed than in Soho.

Rupert Street, 50 Rupert Street, W1. For the more professional set.

King William IV. 77 Hampstead High Street, NW3. Handy for the Heath.

Wine and cocktail bars

American Bar. Savoy Hotel, Strand, WC2. Classic cocktails. Jacket and tie.

Bar des Amis du Vin. 11–13 Hanover Place, WC2. Atmospheric basement with solid wine list and decent French snacks.

Boot and Flogger. 20 Redcross Way, SE1. Club-like wine bar with leather armchairs a short walk from Tate Modern.

Cork and Bottle. 44–46 Cranbourne Street, WC2. Casual basement bar, excellent retreat from Leicester Square.

Corney and Barrow. 116 St Martin's Lane, WC2. Pleasant wine bar at ground level, champagne bar in basement.

El Vino. 47 Fleet Street, EC4. Legendary journalists' haunt now taken over by lawyers. Stuffy dress code.

Gordons. 47 Villiers Street, WC2. Venerable dive close to Covent Garden offering good-value wine, port and Madeira.

Julie's Wine Bar. 137 Portland Road, Holland Park, W11. Bohemian haunt in 1970s and still has Gothic charm.

Truckles of Pied Bull Yard. Bury Place, WC1. Attractive, with open courtyard. Close to British Museum.

Windows. Hilton Hotel, Park Lane, W1. The draw is the view from the 28th floor. Hefty admission charge after 11pm.

NIGHTLIFE

If you're under 30 years old and believe the hype, London is one of the best places to party in the world. But not all nightlife in the capital is dance-till-dawn. Older swingers can enjoy dinner dances, drinking bars, casinos and smart nightclubs.

Despite the boost to its nightlife given by more liberal licensing laws, London is handicapped by rotten public transport. Last Underground trains can leave before midnight, all-night buses are infrequent, and taxis are very expensive.

Yet London remains the clubbing capital of Europe, with hundreds of clubs offering just about every variety of current dance music. Most clubs don't get going until 10pm or 11pm and some will keep going until public transport starts again. Many cater for different clientele (e.g. gays, hip-hop devotees) on different nights. *Time Out* magazine remains the best guide to what's on in any given week.

DANCE CLUBS

Cargo. 83 Rivington Street, EC2 (7739 3440).Varied music in Old Street area.
Electric Ballroom. 184 Camden High Street, NW1 (7485 9006). Eclectic music policy, from rock and hip-hop to jazz.
Fabric. 77A Charterhouse Street, EC1. (7336 8898). Fashionable purpose-built Clerkenwell club; good underground DJs.
Fridge. Town Hall Parade, Brixton Hill, SW2 (7326 5100). Huge dance floor and legendary Saturday gay nights.
Heaven. The Arches, Craven Street, WC2 (7930 2020). Mammoth, popular gay club underneath Charing Cross station.
Hippodrome. Leicester Square, W1 (7437 4311). Wide age range, top 40 music, more popular with tourists than with locals.
Marquee. The N1 Centre, 16 Parkfield Street, N1 (7288 4400). Purpose-built 1,000-capacity Islington venue, with grill room and occasional circus acts.
Ministry of Sound. 103 Gaunt Street, SE1 (7378 6528). As much a brand as a club

but still popular. Near Elephant & Castle.
Subterania. 12 Acklam Street, W10 (8960 4590). Ladbroke Grove club noted for its R&B nights.
Turnmills. 63 Clerkenwell Road (7250 3409). Older mixed clubbers. All-night.
www.schooldisco.com runs music nights at various locations for clubbers eager to dress up in school uniform.

NIGHTCLUBS

Browns. 4 Great Queen Street, WC1 (7831 7899). Old-style opulence for new-style celebs. Tries to be 'exclusive'.
Café de Paris. 3 Coventry Street, W1 (7734 7700). Spacious, glamorous celebrity haunt. Modern British cuisine.
Madame Jo-Jo's. 8–10 Brewer Street, W1 (7734 3040). Las Vegas glitz meets high-camp drag acts.
Stringfellow's. 16–19 Upper St Martin's Lane, WC2 (7240 5534). In the ageing Playboy tradition, with added lap dancing.

COMEDY CLUBS

There are more than 100 venues, many in pubs. The best-known clubs are:
Comedy Store. 1A Oxendon Street, SW1 (7344 0234). Many big names started here.
Jongleurs. Venues at Camden (Dingwalls Building, Chalk Farm Road, Camden Lock) and Battersea (The Cornet, 49 Lavender Gardens, SW11). Tel: 0870-7870707. Camden also has disco dancing.

CASINOS

There are around two dozen in central London. The best-known are:
Aspinalls. 28 Curzon Street, W1 (7499 4599).
Crockfords Club. 30 Curzon Street, W1 (7493 7771).
Golden Nugget. 23–32 Shaftesbury Avenue, W1 (7439 0009).
Ritz Club. 150 Piccadilly, W1 (7499 1818).
Sportsman Club. 40 Bryanston Street, W1 (7414 0061).

DIARY OF ANNUAL EVENTS

JANUARY
London International Boat Show, Earl's Court: the world's largest.
Charles I Commemoration (last Sunday): English Civil War Society parade as Royalists from Charles I's statue in Whitehall to his place of execution outside Banqueting House.
FEBRUARY
Chinese New Year: colourful parade centring on Gerrard Street in Soho.
MARCH
Ideal Home Exhibition, Earl's Court. New ideas and products for the home.
London Book Fair, Olympia.
Chelsea Antiques Fair, Old Town Hall, Kings Road, SW3.
Easter Parade, Battersea Park. Carnival floats and fancy dress.
Camden Jazz Festival, Camden Town. Music, dance, film.
APRIL
Oxford and Cambridge Boat Race: annual Thames race held since 1856 between university oarsmen between Putney and Mortlake.
London Marathon: thousands run from Greenwich Park to Westminster.
MAY
Chelsea Flower Show, Royal Hospital, SW3. Major horticultural show and social event. Details: 7834 4333.
JUNE
Beating Retreat, Horse Guards Parade, Whitehall. Annual ceremonial display of military bands.
Royal Academy Summer Exhibition, Burlington House, Piccadilly. Work by professional and amateur artists. Until August. Works for sale.
Trooping the Colour, The Queen's official birthday celebrated with a royal procession along the Mall to Horse Guards Parade.
Grosvenor House Antiques Fair, Grosvenor House Hotel, Park Lane. A large and prestigious event.

Wimbledon Lawn Tennis Championships, All England Club. World-famous two weeks of tennis.
JULY
Henry Wood Promenade Concerts, Royal Albert Hall. Series of classical concerts known as The Proms.
Royal Tournament, Earl's Court. Military displays from the Royal Army, Navy and Air Force.
AUGUST
Notting Hill Carnival, Ladbroke Grove (bank holiday weekend): colourful and lively West Indian street carnival (Europe's largest).
SEPTEMBER
Chelsea Antiques Fair, Old Town Hall, King's Road, SW3: contact tel: 01444-482514.
OCTOBER
Costermongers' Pearly Harvest Festival (1st Sun), Church of St Martin-in-the-Fields, Trafalgar Square.
NOVEMBER
London to Brighton Veteran Car Run (1st Sunday): hundreds of venerable vehicles start out from Hyde Park and head south.
Lord Mayor's Show: procession, with gilded coach, from the Guildhall in the City to Strand.
State Opening of Parliament, House of Lords, Westminster. The Queen arrives in a state coach.
Guy Fawkes Day (5 November): bonfires and fireworks celebrate failure to blow up Parliament in 1605.
Christmas Lights: switched on in Oxford and Regent streets.

DECEMBER
Olympia International Horse Show, Olympia: major international show jumping championships.
New Year's Eve, Trafalgar Square: thousands congregate and sing Auld Lang Syne at midnight.

SHOPPING

For those wanting the best of European and International designer fashions, **Knightsbridge**, home to the high-class department stores Harrods and Harvey Nichols, has the highest concentration of such shops. Haute couture names from Armani to Yves Saint Laurent sit next to established British designers Katharine Hamnett, Anya Hindmarch and Bruce Oldfield.

Old Bond Street and **New Bond Street**, in Mayfair, also offer a vast choice of designer labels. **Savile Row**, again in Mayfair, specialises in bespoke tailoring, and **Cork Street** in commercial art galleries.

In the **Piccadilly** area, you'll find the upmarket grocer's Fortnum and Mason, as well as some of London's oldest shops, many of which hold royal warrants to supply the Queen and her family with goods. Nearby **Jermyn Street** specialises in shirts. **Regent Street** is home to Britain's largest toy shop, Hamleys, and London institution Liberty.

High-street chains and department stores characterise **Oxford Street**, the capital's main shopping thoroughfare. Nearby **Tottenham Court Road** is dominated by electronics stores and interiors shops.

Although **Soho** has never quite lost its seedy image, between the sex shops are some great fashion boutiques selling hip urbanwear. Bookworms should head to **Charing Cross Road**, renowned for its second-hand and antiquarian bookshops.

Covent Garden is one of London's more laid-back areas, with shops ranging from high-street and cutting-edge fashion boutiques to quirky specialist places selling everything from teapots to kites. It is most famous, though, for its market, which has held a licence since 1678.

Although the **King's Road** is no longer the destination for leading fashions, shoppers still flock to it for its popular chain stores and small boutiques. **Kensington Church Street** is a favourite destination of antiques lovers, with more than 80 dealers lining the street. **Notting Hill**, famous for its Portobello market, also has many fashionable boutiques.

Museum shops

All the major museums and galleries, such as the Victoria and Albert and the Natural History Museum, sell unusual and innovative merchandise, sometimes tied in with exhibitions. You don't always need to visit the museums themselves: the British Museum has shops in Bloomsbury Street, WC1, and at Heathrow Terminal 4, and the Science Museum has a concession at Selfridges department store in Oxford Street.

Where to find it

DEPARTMENT STORES

The Conran Shop
81 Fulham Road, SW3
Terence Conran's first design mecca, in Michelin's former London HQ, a glorious 1905 art nouveau building.

Dickins & Jones
224–44 Regent Street, W1
Great beauty and lingerie sections. Personal shopping service available.

Fenwick
63 New Bond Street Street, W1
Top concessions (Armani, etc), good accessories and best toilets in the area.

Harrods
Knightsbridge, SW1
'Everything for everybody everywhere' is the motto of this lavish institution. Scruffy customers not admitted.

Harvey Nichols
67 Brompton Road, SW3
The latest designer collections, good perfume and food departments, fashionable Fifth Floor Café.

John Lewis
278–306 Oxford Street, W1
Competitively priced fashion, haberdashery, hardware and electrical goods.

Liberty
214 Regent Street, W1
From Arts and Crafts trendsetter to contemporary icon. Stylish homeware, fabrics, fashion in Tudor-style building.

Lillywhite's
24–36 Regent Street, W1
London's largest sports shop. Prices are high but service is good.

Marks & Spencer
458 Oxford Street, W1
Flagship of the much improved chain. Still great for underwear but also catwalk-led designs plus good food hall.

Selfridges & Co
400 Oxford Street, W1
London's hippest department store, towards the western end of Oxford Street.

Fashion & Footwear

All the big-names, from Agnès B to Zara, have shops in London, generally in Oxford Street, Regent Street, Knightsbridge and South Kensington.

Bertie Wooster
284 Fulham Road, SW10
Alluring vintage clothes for men: dinner jackets, Savile Row suits, cufflinks.

Burberry
21–3 New Bond Street, W1
For the classic traditional house check.

Jimmy Choo
169 Draycott Avenue, SW1
Beautiful, sexy creations, celebrated for their daringly high heels.

Mulberry
41–2 New Bond Street, W1
Ttraditional British design with a contemporary twist. New Bond Street itself is a showcase of designer names.

Paul Smith
43 Floral Street, WC2
Cutting-edge designer clothes for men and women, right in Covent Garden.

Sweaty Betty
35 Heath Street, Hampstead NW3
Women's sports gear that flatters too.

Jewellery & Watches

Butler & Wilson
189 Fulham Road, SW3
Fabulous costume jewellery, diamanté tiaras, butterfly brooches, vintage handbags. (Also at 20 South Molton St, W1.)

Cartier
175–6 New Bond Street, W1
Wood surroundings, elegant jewels.

Tiffany & Co.
25 Old Bond Street, W1
You can get a key-ring for £40, but most items cost rather more.

Watches of Switzerland
16 New Bond Street, W1
Prices start at £500 for the big names – Piaget, Patek Phillipe, etc.

Health & Beauty

Jo Malone
150 Sloane Street, SW3
Stylishly presented, delicately scented toiletries from the acclaimed beautician.

Neal's Yard Remedies
15 Neal's Yard, WC2
Alternative health shop ranging from aromatherapy blends to baby products.

Space.NK Apothecary
4 Thomas Neal Centre, Earlham Street, WC1, and various branches
Patronised by Madonna, this store has a wide range of cult beauty products.

Gifts & Souvenirs

Asprey & Garrard
167 New Bond Street, W1
Seriously expensive sterling silver and jewellery. Favourite for wedding gifts.

The Man Who Has Everything
77 Parsons Green Lane, Fulham, SW6
Funky gadgets such as cognac warmers.

Octopus
28 Carnaby Street, W1
Bright, often witty designs in bags, watches, jewellery, umbrellas, ties...

FOOD & DRINK

Fortnum & Mason
181 Piccadilly, W1
London's glamorous grocer is a visual treat. Good for English gourmet gifts.

Justerini & Brooks
61 St James's Street, SW1
Top range of fine wines and whiskys.

Thornton's
353 Oxford Street, W1
Speciality chocolates, great ice cream.

CHILDREN

Benjamin Pollock's Toyshop
44 The Market, Covent Garden, WC2
Amazing range of old-fashioned toys.

Hamleys
188–96 Regent Street, W1
The world's largest toy shop has seven magical floors for kids.

Mothercare
461 Oxford Street, W1
Essentials for babies, pre-schoolers. Lots of branches (tel: 08453-304030).

SPECIALIST

Anything Left-Handed
57 Brewer Street, Soho, W1
Scissors, cutlery, corkscrews and more for those of a sinister bent.

The Button Queen
19 Marylebone Lane, W1
Lots of antique and modern buttons.

The Dolls House Company
The Market Place, WC2
Everything for miniature home-owners.

Legends Boardriders
119–21 Oxford Street, W1
Heaven for skate-and surfboarders.

Stanford's
12–14 Long Acre, WC2
Tops for maps and travel guides.

Vintage Magazine Shop
39–43 Brewer Street, Soho, W1
A cardboard cutout of Harrison Ford or Marilyn Monroe? They've got it.

Woof Woof
178a King's Road, SW3
For pampering pooches and pussycats.

● *Insight Guide: Shopping in London is a 128-page pocket-size book packed with hundreds of detailed listings, plus advice and background features.*

London's best markets

● **BERWICK STREET**, Soho, W1. 8am– 6pm Mon–Sat. Good-value fruit, vegetables, cheese, bread, spices.
● **BOROUGH MARKET**, Southwark Street, SE1. Noon–6pm Fri, 9am–4pm Sat. Imaginative farmers'market, lots of organic produce.
● **BRICK LANE**, E1. 8am–1pm Sun. Everything from bananas to bicycles. Great fun.
● **BRIXTON MARKET**, Electric Avenue, SW9. African and Caribbean produce plus secondhand clothes and bric a brac.
● **CAMDEN LOCK**, off Chalk Farm Road, NW1. Outdoor 10am–6pm Sat–Sun, indoor 10am–6pm Tues–Sun. Tourist-packed crafts market in canalside setting. Stalls in nearby **CAMDEN MARKET** (Camden High Street, 9am–5.30pm Thurs–Sun) have street fashion and retro gear.
● **COLUMBIA ROAD**, Bethnal Green, E2. The best flower market. 8am–1pm Sun.
● **GREENWICH MARKET**, Greenwich High Road, SE10. 9am–5pm Sat–Sun. Arts and crafts, secondhand clothes, books, records.
● **JUBILEE MARKET, APPLE MARKET**, Covent Garden Piazza, WC2. The first is a souvenir trap for tourists, the second has jewellery.
● **PETTICOAT LANE**, Middlesex Street, E1. 9am–2pm Sun. Crowded tradtional market selling everything from food to hardware.
● **PORTOBELLO ROAD**, W11. Antiques market 7am–6pm Sat; general market Mon–Sat, closed Thurs afternoon. High-priced antiques, bargain fruit and vegetables, plus wide range of new and secondhand clothes.

PRACTICAL INFORMATION

Getting There

BY AIR

London has two major international airports: Heathrow, 15 miles (24 km) to the west (mainly scheduled flights); and Gatwick, 24 miles (40 km) to the south (scheduled and charter flights). The smaller airports of Stansted and Luton are north of London. There is also the tiny London City Airport in Docklands, used by small aircraft flying mainly to European cities.

HEATHROW AIRPORT

The fastest way into London is the **Heathrow Express** to Paddington Station, which runs every 15 minutes and takes 15 minutes. The fare is a hefty £13 (US$20) single – possibly the world's costliest rail ticket per mile.

There is also a direct **Underground** route (£3.60 single), on the Piccadilly Line, which reaches the West End in around 40 minutes. Keep your ticket: you'll need it to exit the system. For London Underground enquiries, tel: 7222 1234.

London Regional Transport (LRT) runs an **Airbus** service with red double-decker and single-decker buses picking up from all terminals. Buses leave every 30 minutes from 6.30am to 10.15pm daily, take up to an hour and stop near major hotels on the way. A single fare of £6 can be bought from the driver. For 24-hour Airbus travel information, tel: 7222 1234.

Heathrow is also well-served for **taxis**. A ride into town in a familiar London 'black cab' will cost from £30 plus tip, depending on destination.

GATWICK AIRPORT

Trains and coaches run to London's Victoria Station. The **Gatwick Express** leaves every 15 minutes from 5am to midnight then hourly through the night. It takes 30 minutes and costs around £11 one-way. Children under four years old travel free; children aged between five and 15 travel for half of the adult fare. Gatwick Express Information, tel: 0990-301 530.

Connex SouthCentral has cheaper fares on its trains to Victoria station. Thameslink runs trains to four London stations: Kings Cross, Farringdon, Blackfriars and London Bridge.

Flightline 777 coaches leave from both the North and South terminals and take about 70 minutes to reach Victoria (traffic is heavy). A single fare is £7.50.

LUTON AIRPORT

Luton Airport, north of London, is connected by **Thameslink** rail services via King's Cross and Blackfriars. There is a shuttle bus between the station and the airport. The journey to King's Cross takes about 40 minutes and runs every 20 minutes. **Green Line** coach services also run via Victoria station (tel: 0345-788 788) and take about 90 minutes.

> ### The Channel Tunnel
> The Channel Tunnel provides Eurostar passenger services by rail from Paris Nord (3 hours, Eurostar Paris, tel: 33 1-49 70 01 75) and Brussels Midi (2 hours 40 minutes, Eurostar Brussels, tel: 32 2-322 5259) to London's Waterloo. UK Eurostar bookings, tel: 0990 186 186, for bookings in the UK from abroad, tel: (44) 1233-617 775. In the US call 1-800-eurostar or 1-800 356 66711.
> Sea services operate between 12 British and over 20 Continental ports. The shortest ferry crossing time from the Continent is about one hour 30 minutes, from Calais to Dover.

STANSTED AIRPORT

A direct rail link goes to London's Liverpool Street Station every half-hour; journey time of 45 minutes. **Flightline** coaches run every hour between Victoria and Stansted.

LONDON CITY AIRPORT

A dozen carriers run services to and from 18 European cities. "Shuttlebus" services connect the airport with Canary Wharf Underground station, and Canning Town interchange station. For flight enquiries, tel: 020-7646 0000; www.londoncityairport.com.

Getting Around

Central London is surprisingly compact and, for short journeys, it's almost almost quicker to walk, armed with a good map. (We recommend *Insight FlexiMap: London*; being laminated, it's weatherproof and easy to fold.)

UNDERGROUND

The Underground ('Tube'), although ageing and creaking, is the quickest way to get around central London. Trains run from 5.30am (Sunday 7.30am) to just before midnight. Prices vary by distance according to a zoning system and tickets may be bought from a booking office or machine. A single ticket in Zone 1, central London, is £1.60 (around US$2.50). A carnet of 10 tickets is worth buying at £11.50.

● *See map on inside back cover.*

OVERGROUND TRAINS

If you are staying in the suburbs, the fastest way into central London is often by the spaghetti-like rail network used intensively by commuters but relatively quiet between rush hours. Ask for advice locally. See panel below for details of where the trains terminate.

BUSES

There are 129 red bus routes, numbered up to 300. They run between 6.30am and 11pm. The quicker Red Arrow buses are usually single-deckers, numbered from 500. They call only at stops serving main shopping

London's Railway Termini

These are the city's principal mainline stations, with the areas they serve:

● **Charing Cross Station.** Services to south London and southeast England: Canterbury, Folkestone, Hastings, Dover Priory.

● **Euston Station.** Services to northwest London and beyond to Birmingham and the northwest: Liverpool, Manchester, Glasgow.

● **King's Cross Station.** Services to north London and beyond to the northeast: Leeds, York, Newcastle, Edinburgh and Aberdeen.

● **St Pancras Station.** For points not quite so far north, such as Nottingham, Derby, Sheffield.

● **Liverpool Street Station & Fenchurch Street.** Services to east and northeast London, Cambridge and East Anglia.

● **Paddington Station.** Services to west London and beyond to Oxford, Bath, Bristol, the west, and Wales.

● **Victoria Station.** Services to south London and southeast England, including Gatwick airport, Brighton, Newhaven and Dover.

● **Waterloo Station.** Mainly commuter services to southwest London, Southampton, and southern England as far as Exeter, including Richmond, Windsor and Ascot. The international Eurostar service also operates from here with regular services to Brussels and Paris; both can be visited as day trips.

● **Other termini,** such as Marylebone, London Bridge, Cannon Street and Blackfriars, are mainly commuter stations.

Train services are run by a variety of private companies. For information on times for any destination in the UK, tel: 0345 48 49 50.

centres and stations. An all-night (but less frequent) service runs between the centre and the outer suburbs. A book of six bus tickets costs £3.90.

TRAVEL PASSES

A one-day Travelcard offers more or less unlimited use of the red buses and the Underground in the central zones and is good value for £4. A 7-day card costs £18.90 and requires a passport-style photograph.

TAXIS

A taxi may be hailed if the yellow 'For Hire' sign is lit. The black cabs (other colours are possible) are licensed and their drivers have an encyclopaedic knowledge of London's roads. But fares are high, especially at night (fortunately, many accept credit cards). A tip of at least 10 percent is expected. You can also telephone for a black cab: 7272 0272 or 7253 5000.

TOURS

Bus tours

A good introduction to the sights of London are the tours on double-decker buses with English-speaking guides or taped commentaries in various languages. Just turn up at a departure point such as Marble Arch or Trafalgar Square. Most tickets allow you to hop on and off at various points.

Operators include **The Big Bus Company** (tel: 7233 9533) and **The Original London Sightseeing Tour** (tel: 8877 1722).

Walking tours

These are an ideal way of getting to get to know London in the company of a qualified guide. **Original London Walks** (tel: 7624 3978) has almost 100 walks, many with literary and historical themes. Other operators include **Historical Tours** (020-8668 4019), **Stepping Out** (020-8881 2933) and **Streets of London** (07812-501418).

Black Taxi Tours of London

These offer a full commentary from knowledgeable cabbies. Tours are two hours long. Drivers will pick up from and deliver back to hotels. Cost £70 (approx US$100 or 112 euros) per cab – up to five passengers. 24-hour booking: 7289 4371.

River travel

Much of London's history was centred on the Thames and seeing the city from the river provides a fascinating perspective. **City Cruises** (tel: 7237 5134) serves the main piers down to Tower Pier and Greenwich; **Westminster and Greenwich Cruises** (tel: 7930 4097) runs tours from Westminster Pier to Greenwich; and **Catamaran Cruises** (tel: 7839 3572) operates from Embankment and Tower piers to Greenwich.

Canal trips

Jason's Trip (tel: 7286 3428) is a traditional painted narrow boat making 90-minute trips along the Regent's Canal between Little Venice and Camden Lock, Apr–Oct. **London Waterbus Company** (tel: 7482 2550) runs from Camden Lock to Little Venice with discounted tickets to the zoo at Regent's Park.

Facts for the Visitor

TRAVEL DOCUMENTS

To enter the UK, you need a valid passport (or any form of official identification if a citizen of the European Union). Commonwealth citizens, Americans, EU nationals or citizens of most other European and South American countries don't need visas.

CURRENCY

The pound sterling (£) is divided into 100 pence and is worth around US$1.50 or 1.6 euros. Many of London's large stores have converted their tills to accept both pounds and euros.

PUBLIC HOLIDAYS

1 January (New Year's Day), Good Friday, Easter Monday, the first Monday in May (May Day), the last Monday in May (Spring Bank Holiday), the last Monday in August, Christmas Day, Boxing Day.

HEALTH PROBLEMS

European Union citizens can receive free treatment on production of an E111 form. Citizens of other countries must pay – except for emergency treatment, which is always free.

Major hospitals include Charing Cross Hospital (Fulham Palace Road, W6, tel: 8846 1234); St Mary's (Praed Street, W2 (tel: 7886 6666); and St Thomas's (Lambeth Palace Road, SE1, tel: 7928 9292). Guy's Hospital Dental Department is at St Thomas Street, SE1, tel: 7955 4317.

To find the nearest hospital or doctor's surgery, tel: 0800-665 544.

Late pharmacy: Bliss Chemist at 5 Marble Arch W1 opens until midnight.

LOST PROPERTY

If you leave anything on a bus or on the Underground, enquire in person at the London Transport Lost Property Office, 200 Baker Street (Mon–Fri 9.30am–2pm). For articles lost in taxis, try the Metropolitan Police Lost Property Office, 15 Penton Street, N1 (Mon–Fri 9am–4pm; tel: 7833 0996).

MEDIA

Newspapers

National papers include the *Daily Telegraph* and *The Times* (on the right politically), *The Independent* (in the middle), and *The Guardian* (left of centre). Most have Sunday equivalents. The *Financial Times* is dominant in its field. Except for the *Daily Mirror*, the tabloids (*The Sun, The Star, Daily Mail* and *Daily Express)* are conservative. The *Evening Stan-*

dard (Mon–Fri) is good for cinema and theatre listings. Foreign newspapers and magazines are sold at many newsstands and at main railway stations.

Listings magazines

Supreme in this field is the long-established weekly *Time Out*, but the *Evening Standard* includes a free listings magazine on Thursdays.

Television

BBC1 and BBC2 are financed by annual TV licences; ITV, Channel 4 (C4) and Five are funded solely by advertising. There are scores of cable and satellite channels. Many hotels will offer BBC News 24 and CNN.

Radio

BBC stations include Radio 1 (98.8fm, pop), Radio 2 (89.2fm, easy listering), Radio 3 (91.3fm (classical music, drama), Radio 4 (93.5fm, current affairs, plays), BBC London (94.9fm, music, chat) and BBC World Service (648 kHz, news). The many commercial stations include LBC (97.3fm, talk), Capital FM (96.8fm, pop), Jazz FM (102.2fm), and Classic FM (100.9fm).

SPORTS FACILITIES

Golf: Contact the English Golf Union (www.englishgolfunion.org; tel: 01526-354 500) for details of courses. Regent's

> ### Telephones
> London's UK dialling code is 020. To call from abroad, dial the 44 international access code for Britain, then 20, then the eight-digit number. To call abroad from London, dial 00, then the country code (e.g. 1 for North America, 353 for Ireland). The international operator is on 155.
>
> If using a US credit phone card, first dial the company's access number: Sprint, tel: 0800-890 877; MCI, tel: 0800-890 222; AT&T, tel: 0800-890 011.
>
> ● For police, fire, ambulance, dial 999.

Park Golf & Tennis School (tel: 7724 0643, has a driving range.

Horse-riding: Hyde Park Stables (tel: 7723 2813) can arrange rides.

Tennis: many local parks have bookable courts. The Lawn Tennis Association (www.lta.org.uk; tel: 7381 7000) has a leaflet on grass courts.

Sports Centres, which often include gyms and swimming pools, include:
Chelsea Sports Centre, Chelsea Manor Street, SW3. Tel: 7352 6985.

Michael Sobell Leisure Centre, Hornsey Road, Holloway, N7. Tel: 7609 2166.

Oasis Sports Centre, 32 Endell Street, WC2. Tel: 7831 1804.

Queen Mother Sports Centre, 223 Vauxhall Bridge Road, SW1. Tel: 7630 5522.

Westway Sports Centre, 1 Crowthorne Road, W10. Tel: 8969 0992.

TOURIST INFORMATION

The Britain Visitor Centre, 1 Regent Street, Piccadilly Circus, is the central source of tourist information. It has an accommodation and theatre booking service, a bookshop and bureau de change. There are 19 other smaller centres in Greater London, including one on Victoria Station forecourt and another in the arrivals hall at Waterloo International Terminal.

If you're abroad, check the site www.visitbritain.com, write to the British Tourist Authority at Thames Tower, Black's Road, London W6 8EL, or contact one of these BTA offices:

Australia: Level 16, Gateway, 1 Macquarie Place, Sydney, NSW 2000. Tel: 02-9377 4400. Fax: 02-9377 4499.

Canada: Suite 120, 5915 Airport Road, Mississauga, Ontario, L4V1T1. Tel: (905) 405 1840. Fax: (905) 405 1835.

New Zealand: 3rd Floor, Dilworth Building, Queen/Customs Street, Auckland 1. Tel: 9-303 1446. Fax: 9-377 6965.

Singapore: Cecil Court, 138 Cecil Street, Singapore 069 538. Tel: 65-227 5400. Fax: 65-227 5411.

South Africa: Lancaster Gate, Hyde Lane, Hyde Park, Sandton 2196. Tel: 11-325 0342. Fax: 11-325 0344.

United States. Chicago: 625 N. Michigan Avenue, Suite 1510, Chicago, IL 60611-1977. Tel: (312) 787-0464. Fax: (312) 787-9641. **Los Angeles:** 11661 San Vicentre Blvd, Los Angeles, CA 90049. Tel: (310) 820-4206. Fax: (310) 820-4406. **New York:** 7th Floor, 551 Fifth Avenue, New York, NY 10176-0799. Tel: (212) 986-2266. Fax: (212) 986-1188.

INTERNET CAFES

London has many internet cafés. The most widespread is the EasyEverything chain which has mega cafés in Victoria, Oxford Street, Trafalgar Square, Tottenham Court Road and Kensington, all open 24 hours a day. www.easyeverything.com

Other smaller cyber cafés include Webshak in Soho, Cyberia in Whitfield Street, W1, Offshore Café behind Piccadilly Circus in Sackville Street. You can also surf at Waterstone's bookshop in Piccadilly.

USEFUL WEBSITES

www.insightguides.com includes comprehensive hotel listings for London.
www.londontouristboard.co.uk This London Tourist Board and Convention Bureau site has information on hotels, restaurants, pubs and attractions.
www.thisislondon.com This site, maintained by the *Evening Standard* newspaper, has detailed listings of events.
www.netlondon.com Internet directory. Links to hotels, museums, theatres.
london.hotelguide.net A comprehensive guide to London's accommodation.
www.londononline.co.uk Up-to-date going-out information. Trendy.
www.travelbritain.com/london/tourism A site for basic travel information.
www.bbc.co.uk Gigantic site includes world news and UK what's on guide.

ACCOMMODATION

● **Our website, insightguides.com, lists hundreds of hotels in London. All listings give detailed descriptions and many include photographs.**

In accordance with supply and demand, rooms are small and prices are high. Victoria, London's traditional hotel district, has some delightfully old-fashioned hotels in most price brackets, and the streets close to Victoria Station are full of terraced bed-and-breakfast accommodation. The second big area – around Kensington High Street, Earl's Court and the Gloucester Road – has medium-range hotels of dependable comfort and, at least, some style.

The top West End hotels are for the seriously wealthy and the bottom end of the price range can be very humble. The Bloomsbury area is a good choice: it's central, has reasonable prices, and retains some dignity, even romance.

The area roughly between Edgware Road, Bayswater Road, Paddington and Queensway, is full of hotels. Quality and prices vary enormously but the area is convenient for the West End and Queensway has plenty of bustle.

The listings below are arranged into price brackets. The categories are based on one night's accommodation for one person, exclusive of breakfast. Many hotels offer special deals at weekends and outside peak season, so it is always worth checking.

£	under £100
££	£100–£150
£££	£150–£200
££££	over £200

TOP CLASS HOTELS

Berkeley Hotel. Wilton Place, SW1. Tel: 7235 6000. Fax: 7235 6000. Low-key, seldom advertised. A country-house feel. Swimming pool. **££££**

Claridge's. Brook Street, W1. Tel: 7629 8860. Fax: 7499 2210. Has long had a reputation for dignity and graciousness. **££££**

Dorchester. Park Lane, W1. Tel: 7629 8888. Fax: 7495 7342. Very expensive indeed. Lovely views over Hyde Park. **££££**

Lanesborough. 1 Lanesborough Place, SW1. Tel: 020 7259 5599. Fax: 7259 5606. Deluxe hotel overlooking Hyde Park Corner. Neoclassical facade, opulent Regency-style interior. Most expensive suite: £5,300 a night. **££££**

Savoy. Strand, WC2. Tel: 7836 4343. Fax: 7240 6040 Solid reputation for comfort, and personal service (if a little formal). **££££**

> **Telephone codes**
> If you are telephoning from outside London but from within the UK, prefix the numbers in this section with 020. If you're outside the UK, prefix with 44-20.

LUXURY

Blakes. 33 Roland Gardens, SW7. Tel: 7370 6701. Fax: 7373 0442. Laid-back, cosmopolitan hotel popular with theatrical and media folk. 51 rooms. **£££–££££**

Brown's. 30 Albemarle Street, W1. Tel: 7493 6020. Fax: 7493 9381. Very British, Victorian-style hotel. Smart Mayfair location. 118 rooms. **££££**

The Connaught. 16 Carlos Place, W1. Tel: 7499 7070. Fax: 7495 3262. Discreet but immaculate service, superb decor (if a little gentlemen's club-ish). Only 90 rooms. **££££**

Halcyon. 81 Holland Park, W1. Tel: 7727 7288. Fax: 7229 8516. Former townhouse in west London turned into small hotel with a country-house ambience. **££££**

Landmark London. 222 Marylebone

Road, NW1. Tel: 7631 8000. Fax: 7631 8080. Modern eight-storey building with a glass domed atrium has good-sized rooms. **££££**

Mandarin Oriental. 66 Knightsbridge, SW1. Tel: 7235 2000. Fax: 7201 3633. Sumptuous in a Victorian marble-and-chandeliers style. **££££**

Metropolitan. 19 Old Park Lane, W1. Tel: 7447 1000. Fax: 7447 1100. Christina Ong's attempt to create a New York ambience. **££££**

Montcalm. 34–40 Great Cumberland Place, W1. Tel: 7402 4288. Fax: 7724 9180. Part of an elegant Georgian crescent. 120 rooms. Rather plush. **£££–££££**

Ritz. 150 Piccadilly, W1. Tel: 7493 8181. Fax: 7493 2687. 130 rooms. Not quite what it was, despite refurbishment. **££££**

Royal Garden. 2–24 Kensington High Street, W2.Tel: 7937 8000. Fax: 7361 1991. Kensington's only 5-star hotel. 400 rooms. **££££**

MODERATE

Basil Street Hotel. 8 Basil Street, SW3. Tel: 7581 3311. Fax: 7581 3693. Lots of old-fashioned charm. For those who like a country house atmosphere. Close to Harrods. 90 rooms. **£££**

> **Hotel costs**
> Hotel bills usually include service and no extra tip is needed, but if you wish to repay good service, 10 percent split between the deserving is the custom. Equally, you can insist that service be deducted if you feel you've been treated less than impressively. Ensure when booking that the price quoted is inclusive, and isn't going to be bumped up by a mysterious 'travellers' charge' or other extras on the final bill. If you reserve in advance, you may be asked for a deposit. Reservations made, whether in writing or by phone, are binding contracts.

Cadogan. 75 Sloane Street, SW1. Tel: 7235 7141. Fax: 7245 0994. A 19th-century style hotel, owned by Historic House Hotels. 65 rooms. **£££**

Charing Cross. Strand, WC2. Tel: 7839 7282. Fax: 7839 6685. Next door to Charing Cross rail station and Underground. Comfortable and reliable. **£££**

Goring. 15 Beeston Place, Grosvenor Gardens, SW1. Tel: 7396 9000. Fax: 7834 4393. Delightfully traditional hotel not far from Buckingham Palace. Relaxed atmosphere. **£££–££££**

Hazlitt's. 6 Frith Street, W1. Tel: 7434 1771. Fax: 7438 1524. One of London's oldest houses, dating to 1718, in heart of Soho. 23 rooms, all with bath and all furnished with antiques. **£££**

Hotel Russell. Russell Square, WC1. Tel: 7837 6470. Fax: 7837 2857. Spacious hotel in the heart of Bloomsbury. 328 rooms, all with bath. Meals. **£££**

Mount Royal. Bryanston Street, W1. Tel: 7629 8040. Fax: 7499 7792. Close to Marble Arch. 700 rooms. **£££**

Portobello. 22 Stanley Gardens, W11, Tel: 7727 2777. Fax: 7792 9641. Extravagantly decorated, favoured by movie and rock stars. 24 rooms. **£££**

Rubens. 39–41 Buckingham Palace Road, SW1. Tel: 7834 6600. Fax: 7233 6037. Smart location opposite the Royal Mews, and close to Victoria station. 175 rooms. **£££**

Strand Palace. Strand, WC2. Tel: 0870 400 8702. Fax: 7836 2077. Massive, long-established, London hotel. Good location. 783 rooms. **£££**

INEXPENSIVE

Abbey Court. 20 Pembridge Gardens, W2. Tel: 7221 7518. Fax: 7792 0858. Beautifully restored Notting Hill town house, with the atmosphere of a private home. 22 rooms. **££**

Academy. 21 Gower Street, WC1. Tel: 7631 4115. Fax: 7636 3442. Small and welcoming Bloomsbury

hotel. 48 rooms, 5 with private bath. **££**
Kennedy. 43 Cardington Street, NW1. Tel: 7387 4400. Fax: 7387 5122. Modern air-conditioned hotel next to Euston station. 360 rooms with private bath. **££**
Knightsbridge Green. 159 Knightsbridge, SW1. Tel: 7584 6274. Fax: 7225 1635. Very good value for its area, a family-run hotel. Mostly suites, double and family-sized rooms. 23 rooms, all non-smoking. **££**
Mercure London City Bankside. 75–79 Southwark Street, SE1. Tel: 7902 0800. Fax: 7902 0810. French chain hotel close to Tate Modern and the Globe Theatre. **££**
Norfolk Towers. 34 Norfolk Place, W2. Tel: 7262 3123. Fax: 7224 8687. Elegant hotel with cocktail bar and restaurant. 85 rooms. **££**
Sherlock Holmes. 108 Baker Street, W1. Tel: 7486 6161. Fax: 7486 0884. Handy for Oxford and Regent street shopping. 125 rooms. **££**
Tophams. 28 Ebury Street, SW1. Tel: 7730 8147. 7823 5966. Old-style hotel with faded charm. Good value. **££**
Willett. 32 Sloane Gardens, SW1. Tel: 7824 8415. Fax: 7730 4830. Excellent small hotel with 19 rooms, close to Sloane Square. Very good value. **££**

LEAST EXPENSIVE
Prices usually include breakfast.
Abbey House. 11 Vicarage Gate, W8. Tel: 7727 2594. Fax: 7727 1873. Grand Victorian house. Basic furnishing, but well maintained. 15 rooms, none en suite. **£**
Abcone. 10 Ashburn Gardens, SW7. Tel: 7370 3383. Fax: 7460 3444. Near Kensington High Street. 35 rooms, 26 with bath. **£**
Andrews House. 12 Westbourne Street, W2. Tel: 7723 5365. Fax: 7706 4143. Family-run, in a busy area near Paddington. 17 rooms, 10 with bath. **£**

Bayswater Inn. 8–16 Princes Square, W2. Tel: 7727 8621. Fax: 7727 3346. Close to Portobello Road Market. 127 rooms, all with private bath. **£**
Beverley House. 142 Sussex Gardens, W2. Tel: 7723 3380. Fax: 7262 0324. Well-equipped hotel between Oxford Street and Hyde Park. 23 rooms. **£**
Chester House. 134 Ebury Street, SW1. Tel: 7730 3632. Fax: 7824 8446. B&B accommodation in good location close to Sloane Square. 12 rooms including 2 family-sized. 4 with private bath. **£**
Crescent. 49–50 Cartwright Gardens, WC1. Tel: 7387 1515. Fax: 7383 2054. In quiet Bloomsbury crescent, with private gardens and tennis courts. 27 rooms. **£**
Elizabeth. 37 Eccleston Square, SW1. Tel: 7828 6812. Fax: 7828 6814. A friendly hotel in elegant period square, a few minutes' walk from Victoria Station. 40 rooms, 24 with bath. **£**
Enterprise. 15–25 Hogarth Road, SW5. Tel: 7373 4974. Fax: 7373 5115. Good location close to Kensington High Street. 95 en-suite rooms. **£**
Fielding. 4 Broad Court, Bow Street, WC2. Tel: 7836 8305. Fax: 7497 0064. Compact and charming, quiet location close to Covent Garden. **£**
Georgian House. 35 St George's Drive, SW1. Tel: 7834 1438. Fax: 7976 6085. B&B hotel close to Victoria station. Friendly family atmosphere. 34 rooms, 21 en suite. **£**
Grapevine. 117 Warwick Way, SW1. Tel: 7834 0134. Fax: 7834 7878.

Bed & Breakfasts
Staying in a private home ensures that you meet at least one London family. The **London Bed & Breakfast Agency** specialises in such accommodation, with prices from around £20–£40 a person per night, depending on the area. Tel: 020-7586 2768. Fax: 020-7586 6567. www.londonbb.com

Friendly, privately-owned hotel in Victoria. Good English breakfast. 27 rooms. **££**

Lonsdale. 9–10 Bedford Place, WC1. Tel: 7636 1812. Fax: 7580 9902Old-established B&B with real character in the heart of Bloomsbury. 39 rooms, 1 with private bath. **£**

Mad Hatter. 3–7 Stamford Street, SE1 Tel: 7401 9222. Fax: 7401 7111. Near Tate Modern. Owned by Fuller's pub group. 30 rooms, fair-sized. **£**

Montagu House. 3 Montagu Place, W1. Tel: 7935 4632. Fax: 7486 1443. Well-equipped B&B hotel. 18 rooms (3 with bath). **£**

Oliver Plaza. 33 Trebovir Road, SW5. Tel: 7373 7183. Fax: 7244 6021. B&B hotel with good service and comfortable rooms, all 32 with private bath. Good value. **£**

Regency. 19 Nottingham Place, W1. Tel: 7486 5347. Fax: 7224 6057. Elegantly converted mansion in the heart of the West End. Comfortable. 20 rooms. **£**

Riverside. 23 Petersham Road, Richmond-upon-Thames, Surrey TW10.

> ### 👁 Youth hostels and YMCAs
> The International Youth Hostel Federation (www.yha.org.uk) has beds costing from £16 to £25 in these locations: 36–38 Carter Lane, EC4, near St Paul's (tel: 7236 4965); 38 Boulton Gardens, Earl's Court, SW5 (7373 7083); 4 Wellgarth Road, Golders Green, NW11 (tel: 8458 9054); Holland Walk, Kensington, W8 (tel: 7937 0748); 14 Noel Street, off Oxford Street, W1 (tel: 7734 1618); Island Yard, Salter Road, Rotherhithe, SE16 (tel: 7232 2114); and 79–81 Euston Road, St Pancras, NW1 (tel: 7388 9998).
>
> YMCAs (www.ymca.org.uk) are located at 2 Fann Street, Barbican, EC2 (tel: 7628 0697); 8 Errol Street, near Old Street, EC1 (tel: 7628 8832); and 200 The Broadway, Wimbledon, SW19 (tel: 8542 9055).

Tel: 8940 1339. Fax: 8948 0967. Good Thames views. Handy for Kew Gardens but only a 15-minute rail ride into Waterloo. 22 rooms. **£**

Royal Adelphi. 21 Villiers Street, WC2. Tel: 7930 8764. Fax: 7930 8735. Behind Charing Cross station, a short walk from Covent Garden and theatreland. 47 rooms, 37 with bath. **£**

Strand Continental. 143 Strand, WC2. Tel: 7836 4880. Fax: 7379 6105. Superb location. 23 rooms, none with private bath. No credit cards. **£**

Travel Inns. For value, it's hard to beat Britain's biggest budget hotel chain. There are five Whitbread-owned Travel Inns in central London: at County Hall (by Westminster Bridge), Euston, Kensington (near Earl's Court Tube station), Putney Bridge and Tower Bridge. No frills, but clean and modern and generally around £75 a night. Central reservations: tel: 0870-242 8000. Not surprisingly, they tend to be booked well in advance. **£**

SELF-CATERING APARTMENTS

A family or small group can save money by renting. Some contacts:

Allen House, 8 Allen Street, W8 6BH. Tel: 7938 1346. 42 Kensington flats, 1–3 beds. £1,230–£2,020 a week.

Apartment Services, 2 Sandwich Street, WC1H 9PL. Tel: 7388 3558. 60 flats in central London, particularly Bloomsbury and Covent Garden. £350–£1,700 a week.

Holiday Flats, 1 Princess Mews, Belsize Crescent, NW3 5AP. Tel: 7794 1186. Studio flats to 3-bed flats in Hampstead, St John's Wood and Swiss Cottage. £380–£900 a week.

Holiday Serviced Flats, 273 Old Brompton Road, SW5 9JA. Tel: 7373 4477. Large number of serviced flats in Greater London from £350 weekly for a studio to several thousand pounds for five-star luxury flat.

INDEX

☀ INSIGHT COMPACT GUIDES

Great Little Guides to the following destinations:

Algarve	Finland	Rhodes	Jersey
Amsterdam	Florence	Rio de Janeiro	Lake District
Antigua/Barbuda	French Riviera	Rome	London
Athens	Goa	St. Lucia	New Forest
Bahamas	Gran Canaria	St. Petersburg	North York Moors
Bali	Greece	Salzburg	Northumbria
Bangkok	Holland	Shanghai	Oxford
Barbados	Hong Kong	Singapore	Peak District
Barcelona	Ibiza	Southern Spain	Scotland
Beijing	Iceland	Sri Lanka	Scottish
Belgium	Ireland	Switzerland	Highlands
Berlin	Israel	Sydney	Shakespeare
Bermuda	Italian Lakes	Tahiti	Country
Brittany	Italian Riviera	Tenerife	Snowdonia
Bruges	Jamaica	Thailand	South Downs
Brussels	Jerusalem	Toronto	York
Budapest	Kenya	Turkey	Yorkshire Dales
Burgundy	Laos	Turkish Coast	
California	Lisbon	Tuscany	USA regional:
Cambodia	Madeira	Venice	Boston
Cancún & the	Madrid	Vienna	Cape Cod
Yucatán	Mallorca	Vietnam	Chicago
Chile	Malta	West of Ireland	Florida
Copenhagen	Menorca		Florida Keys
Costa Brava	Milan	UK regional:	Hawaii – Maui
Costa del Sol	Montreal	Bath &	Hawaii – Oahu
Costa Rica	Morocco	Surroundings	Las Vegas
Crete	Moscow	Belfast	Los Angeles
Cuba	Munich	Cambridge &	Martha's Vineyard
Cyprus	Normandy	East Anglia	& Nantucket
Czech Republic	Norway	Cornwall	Miami
Denmark	Paris	Cotswolds	New Orleans
Dominican	Poland	Devon & Exmoor	New York
Republic	Portugal	Edinburgh	San Diego
Dublin	Prague	Glasgow	San Francisco
Egypt	Provence	Guernsey	Washington DC

Insight's checklist to meet all your travel needs:

- **Insight Guides** provide the complete picture, with expert cultural background and stunning photography. Great for travel planning, for use on the spot, and as a souvenir. 186 titles.
- **Insight Museums & Galleries** guides to London, Paris, Florence and New York provide comprehensive coverage of each city's cultural temples and lesser known collections.
- **Insight Pocket Guides** focus on the best choices for places to see and things to do, picked by our correspondents. They include large fold-out maps. More than 130 titles.
- **Insight Compact Guides** are the fact-packed books to carry with you for easy reference when you're on the move in a destination. More than 130 titles.
- **Insight FlexiMaps** combine clear, detailed cartography with essential information and a laminated finish that makes the maps durable and easy to fold. 133 titles.

The world's largest collection of visual travel guides and maps